# YOUR FIRST SPELL JAR (AND 59 MORE...)

MAGICKAL RECIPES FOR THE BEGINNER WITCH TO MANIFEST PROTECTION, PROSPERITY, HAPPINESS, MONEY, POWER, SUCCESS & LOVE (USING CRYSTALS, HERBS, CANDLES, OILS & MORE)

ALLEGRA GRANT

GO PUBLISHING

# CONTENTS

| | |
|---|---|
| Introduction | 1 |
| 1. Spell Jars | 5 |
| 2. Everything You Need To Prepare Your Spells | 19 |
| 3. Casting Your First Spell | 38 |
| 4. Love and Friendship Spells | 54 |
| 5. Spells for Prosperity and Wealth | 60 |
| 6. Protection Spells | 68 |
| 7. Success Spells | 73 |
| 8. Tranquility Spells | 81 |
| 9. Health Spells | 88 |
| 10. Banishment Spells | 98 |
| 11. Blessings | 109 |
| 12. Chakra Healing Spells | 119 |
| About the Author | 129 |
| Ingredients Glossary | 131 |
| Resources | 141 |

© **Copyright Allegra Grant 2022 - All rights reserved.**

The content contained within this book may not be reproduced, duplicated or transmitted without direct written permission from the author or the publisher.

Under no circumstances will any blame or legal responsibility be held against the publisher, or author, for any damages, reparation, or monetary loss due to the information contained within this book. Either directly or indirectly. You are responsible for your own choices, actions, and results.

**Legal Notice:**

This book is copyright protected. This book is only for personal use. You cannot amend, distribute, sell, use, quote or paraphrase any part, or the content within this book, without the consent of the author or publisher.

**Disclaimer Notice:**

Please note the information contained within this document is for educational and entertainment purposes only. All effort has been executed to present accurate, up-to-date, and reliable, complete information. No warranties of any kind are declared or implied. Readers acknowledge that the author is not engaging in the rendering of legal, financial, medical or professional advice. The content within this book has been derived from various sources. Please consult a licensed professional before attempting any techniques outlined in this book.

By reading this document, the reader agrees that under no circumstances is the author responsible for any losses, direct or indirect, which are incurred as a result of the use of the information contained within this document, including, but not limited to, — errors, omissions, or inaccuracies.

# INTRODUCTION

"Mom, I have something to tell you."

I could see her face go white across the kitchen table.

"Allegra, you know you can tell me anything."

"Okay, well, um...I've been dabbling in witchcraft."

Mom's eyes widened, and I could see the gears turning in her head. She was trying to come up with her best *supportive-parent* response, even if she was a little freaked out. She took a deep breath.

"Happy Halloween," she said.

It was June.

We burst out laughing.


I presented her with a spell jar. A healing spell, for her surgery in a few days. I wanted to give her a little blessing for a speedy recovery. She had known I was a crystal girl, but I was introducing some much heavier stuff, and I hadn't really talked to her about it yet.

I walked her through the ingredients, and I could tell

she was touched; I had put a lot of thought into the preparation of the spell.

"Is this like your version of saying, 'I'll pray for you'?"

"Exactly!"

"I'll take it with me to the hospital. Thank you."

Then I hopped on my broom and flew off into the night.

Just kidding. Actually, my dad dropped me off at the train station, and I took New Jersey Transit back to the city.

\* \* \*

My name is Allegra. After my recent deep dive into the world of crystals and stones, I couldn't rest until I learned everything I could about this new world of energy and healing. That's how I met my friend Sebastian. I'll tell you more about Sebastian in a minute. But first, let's get to the reason you're here! Let me teach you your first spell jar recipe.

Well, first things first. What even is a spell jar? Well, it's a fun, simple way to set intentions, improve your intuition, and bring lots of benefits to your life just by focusing on what you want more of. It's also very meditative. I love it.

Spell jars are also sometimes called witch bottles. They've got a *looooong* history, which I'll talk more about later, too. I'm going to teach you the way I learned—by trying. Some people are the "research for ages before trying" type. Some people are "just try it and see what happens" type. See if you can guess which one I am!

Don't get me wrong; I've done *so* much research. As soon as I learned what a spell jar was, I couldn't wait to try it! So I looked up a recipe. I gave it a shot. For me, the research came after my first spell jar—I was so excited.

Honestly...I had no idea what I was doing at first! That

opened up a rabbit hole of all kinds of witchy goodness, which I am here to share with you now. This kind of thing takes practice and is part of an ancient tradition passed down over centuries.

If you've never done one before, that's okay. I'm here to make it easy for you. We'll talk more about the components of a spell jar later on, but I've found it's easier to learn by doing. You don't even have to make this first one yet unless you want to. If it would benefit someone in your life, go ahead! If not, you can just look at the recipe as an example. Like a way to dip your toes in the shallow end.

This book is for *anyone*. Anyone who is at all interested in witchcraft, Wicca, healing spells, crystals, herbs, or anything at all related to the world of magick[1]. You don't have to believe in all this stuff for it to work, either. You can use your own intention in all kinds of ways without doing a full deep dive. You can go as deep—or shallow—as you want.

Of all the ways a witch can perform magic, spell jars are my favorite. That's why this book focuses on spell jars in particular. I absolutely love them. They are portable, creative, and just plain fun.

Let me also say that I am in no way an expert witch. I would classify myself as an intermediate witch.

I just really like spell jars because they're so easy and intuitive. I love coming up with my own recipes, so that's why I'm sharing some of my favorites here with you today.

The spell jar recipes in this book are designed to help you start with the very basics. They'll let you hone your craft gradually, so you can get the hang of things fundamentally and then build up from there. Throughout the book, I'll be talking about the reasoning behind all this, but in the meantime, I've broken it down so you can get started right away.

Specifically, the recipes in this book also let you use your intuition to put your own spin on things. I found out there are so many ways to be a witch. The main thing is finding what works for you. And then doing it! The only way to practice is by, well...practicing. Go figure.

So you see, this book is really about making your life better, along with the lives of those around you. And best of all, we're going to learn by *doing*—actually creating jar spells as we go along. To that end, I'll teach you how to create the spell jar I made for my mom in just a little while. It'll be the first one I teach you, and I'll walk you through it so you can learn how to make jar spells, too. Let's dive right in.

---

1. Oh, by the way, a lot of modern practitioner prefer to use the spelling *magick* as opposed to *magic*. There are myriad reasons why, but the primary one is to separate Modern Wicca *magick* from the Vegas-style David Copperfield *magic*. Also there are 6 characters in the word magick, and six is a powerful number to Wiccans. I beg your pardon, in advance, if I use both spellings in this book.

# CHAPTER 1
# SPELL JARS

I first learned about witchcraft at a festival. A really amazing festival just outside the city. My friend Sebastian invited me. And since I'm totally into things like crystals now, I figured it would be an amazing time!

What I didn't know was how that festival would change my life.

It all started when we arrived. I instantly noticed Sebastian's T-shirt, which said *do no harm* next to a really cool symbolic-looking tree design.

I tried really hard not to ask him about it, but I just couldn't stop looking at it.

Eventually, I couldn't help it.

"Um...Sebastian?"

"Yeah?"

"Can I ask what your shirt means?"

Sebastian, as it turns out, is Wiccan. And the shirt is one of the beliefs most Wiccans have in common. This opened a huge conversation about Wicca, what it is, and Sebastian's beliefs.

The day was just beginning, however. Later we ended

up in a booth owned by a woman named Kelsey, who I'll talk about soon. First, though, Sebastian explained to me all the ins and outs of being a full-on Wicca and being a witch.

As it turns out, they are two different things.

Lots of witches, of course, are practicing Wiccans and believe in all the various tenets (there are many). It's not really considered a formal "religion," per se, but it is a system of beliefs with an ancient history and tradition. The word "witch" actually comes from the same root as the word "Wicca," so it's really intertwined.

Lots and lots of people practice Wicca, and have done for centuries, all over the world. Sebastian's belief about "do no harm" is actually part of a longer phrase: "Do no harm and do as you will." The basic meaning is that we should be mindful that everyone—and every*thing*—is connected. Whatever you do to others, you are actually doing to yourself. Since we're all part of the same glorious universe, whatever we send out comes back to us, multiplied. Such a powerful thing to think about.

So it makes sense to try and keep an ethical mindset, from this perspective.

This idea of "do no harm" is actually the main idea behind Wicca. There are lots and lots of smaller details, but the main idea I took away from it is that Wiccans really are just here to try and help the world as best they can. This can mean people, plants, animals, the earth itself…really just the whole world and everything in it.

It's a complex belief system, with lots of different subsets and ways of understanding it. People of all walks of life practice Wicca.

That conversation gave me a lot of questions and thoughts, naturally. I knew I would learn everything I could.

It turns out, though, that there are lots and lots of people who don't really consider themselves a Wiccan but still practice witchcraft. You can create spells and believe in magic without necessarily being Wiccan. The line is a bit fuzzy, which I really like, actually. Everyone can decide how deep they want to go and which parts work best for them, which says a lot about how inclusive the community is.

Personally, I'm more in the casual witch category than the full Wiccan category, although I've definitely learned plenty about Wicca since that day.

In a nutshell, being a witch just means being a person who believes in and practices magic. It's a long history full of brave, wise witches (men and women!) who choose to do no harm to anyone or anything (as best they can), and also try to do some good in the world with their magic. Witches draw on their own inner strength to be and do something in the world that matters, one small action at a time.

You can do this, too, if you want.

You can stay in the shallow end and learn some basic spell techniques to just occasionally dabble in witchcraft, or you can be more like my friend Sebastian and practice a deeper level of Wicca. The choice is yours, but you don't have to make it right away; you can learn a few things first and then decide. You can even start right now.

## DO SPELLS WORK?

By now, you might be asking if spells really work. Like, seriously, it's nice I gave my mom a jar of rocks to take to the hospital. But was it just a big ol' waste of my time?

First of all, no time spent doing something nice for someone else is a waste of my time. That's a big part of my personal practice. Any time anyone does anything to make the world a better place—even a *slightly* better place—it's worth it.

More importantly, though, working with spell jars is just one way you can tap into that mystical part of the universe that isn't really very mystical at all—it's just some basic quantum physics.

For centuries, witches have been kept on the margins of society. They were one of the few people who dared to try things a different way, to think they could take action and see the results. Using the tools available to them, witches knew they could bring about certain outcomes, just by believing in them.

Of course, few people really understood that. They mostly thought it was weird. Or a crime. Or worse. Witches have really gotten a bad rap over the years.

These days, thankfully, times are changing. People everywhere are starting to wake up and realize that the secret to a successful, fulfilling life is in realizing that you really *do* have power to step up and own what happens in your life. It's an innate power that lives in every tree, every rock, every plant, and every person who has ever lived. Or who ever will live.

This energy is in everything, and we can all access it. And all this raw power is there all the time, waiting for us to work with it.

That's what I call magick—knowing we can work with energy. And then doing it.

If you have a different interpretation, that's fine. That one works for me, though, and that's how I'll be using it in this book. However you believe in magick is fine with me.

For our purposes, I'm going to talk about it in terms of energy. People have written thousands and thousands of words on energy, what it is, how it works, and what it is for, but I'm going to keep it pretty simplistic here. We're here to do magick, after all, not take a physics course.

Still, you will want to grasp some basics first.

Basically, energy is found in the empty space in and around and between all things. It's the fact that atoms are really just empty space, by and large. And your mind has the power to influence that empty space.

Change the space, change the atoms. *Poof!* Magic.

Well, okay. It's not always that simple. You have to focus. You have to believe. You have to step back and watch your results happen on their own without trying to manipulate the outcome, even while putting in all the effort you can to help your magic along. You have to trust, deep down, that the best is happening for you, no matter what.

The first step to bringing your dreams into reality starts with knowing you want it.

Then of course, you can work toward it without magic, if you choose. That's a totally viable option for you. Billions of people do that every day—or so they think.

Since every human has the innate power of energy within, they're actually all doing magic without realizing it. All day, every day, you are already doing magic. Any time you set an intention and take action, that's magic. And we all do this, thousands of times per day.

The trouble is, we don't always think about it. We just sorta float along, struggling and hoping for the best. Or we try really, really hard but never seem to get anywhere, because we haven't grasped the fundamental truths that hold up the universe.

That's how I was for the first several decades of my life. Kinda floundering, not really sure.

After I discovered crystals and learned some basic

witchcraft, I finally realized that in everything I do, I have a choice. I don't need a jar spell to do that; it just happens!

Still, sometimes it's good to give your intention a little help. Creating a spell does just that: it gives your intention a little extra support and lets the energy work for you in the background. Then when you put in your own efforts, you've got the full force of the universe behind you.

See, it's not always enough to just say something and assume it'll come true. I have seen people do that before but not always to the best effect. If you say something often enough, it definitely comes true, sooner or later. This is why we need to be careful. If you say something that you're *sure* is true, no doubt in your mind...sooner or later it becomes truth, even if it wasn't before.

But in general, when we really want something, we're not so sure. Humans have a tendency to put a little fear into our wishes every time we say them out loud. We even do this when talking to ourselves. If you mix fear with your words, that fear will get blended with the energy of it, making it much less likely to come true. Or if it does come true, it might be limited or damaged in some way. Spell jars are a way to fix this problem, because you're letting your beliefs be amplified by something outside of you.

When you set a spell and then release the outcome to the universe, you're letting that fear dissipate. Instead of pouring a ton of fear into the situation, you're letting your absolute belief in the situation be handled by the jar, instead of you. It's almost like the "fix it and forget it" version of wishing.

When you create a spell jar, it's like releasing your wishes to the universe and trusting it to take over. This is powerful. And it really works.

That said, creating the jar shouldn't be your *only* action. It's a great first step, but you shouldn't stop there.

If you really, really want something, it's best to give the universe as much help as possible in bringing it about. Sometimes that means doing research. Sometimes it means learning a new skill or talent. Sometimes it means doing the hard emotional labor to work through something or connect with someone or change who you are as a person. Sometimes it means waiting until the time is right, which can take years.

As you create intentions, spells, and actions, you will start to notice your dreams and wishes come true. The more you do this, the more powerful you will feel. It's amazing, frankly.

In my experience, this is the most empowering part of being a witch. Over time, you start to feel like you can do anything, which is an indescribable feeling. When you go from feeling like nothing is in your control to suddenly realizing that you have the power to go out and get anything you want...the only way I can describe it is magical.

So spells do work. It's just that it's your belief in them that actually does the real magick trick. Spells aren't that mystical at all, really, when it comes down to it...although it's way more fun to pretend that it is. Scientifically speaking, spells have just been harnessing energy all along. They've been doing this for centuries, and only now have we realized how it works. Even though witches have been seen as "crazy" or even evil at times, it's actually the belief in the spells that work, more so than the actual spell itself. And the action you take alongside it.

Just like the centuries of witches who came before you, the ones who knew, without a doubt, that if they said something, it would come true, you can cultivate this power. It might take time. It might take dedication. It might take practice. But if I can do it, I know that you definitely can.

Overall, to answer the question about spells and whether they work—it's not the jar full of rocks that does the magic. It's you. You're the container of infinite spaces and reality, so you get to decide which ones you want to bring about!

Since we live in a time where people are (mostly) down with this type of thing, it is so easy to get involved in being a witch. Setting an intention and then watching it come true with your belief is seriously just, well...magical. It still astonishes me every time, not going to lie. But it's always a good kind of surprise. It's the kind of surprised feeling I get when I didn't know I could do something really difficult, but it turns out I can. So can you.

Because it's honestly so hard to believe you're a powerful influencer of space and time, at least when you first start out. When I first learned about all this stuff, I was nervous. I had no clue what I was doing. I kept finding myself going back to my old beliefs, which were pretty disempowered. But I found that, given a little time and practice, I could get the hang of it. Instead of feeling like the whole world was in charge of me (like I always used to do), I started to learn that I could, in fact, make a change in the world. That's when I really started to feel like a real, honest-to-goodness witch.

That, for me, is magick. Knowing *you* are the writer of your own story. Not your mom, not your boss, not the guy on the street who flips you off...none of those people have power over you. You get to choose how to be and react. That's true power.

Of course, those people can still hurt us deeply. We just get to decide what actions we will take now, as we move into the future. That is also true power.

Spell jars are only one way to harness this power. But they're super fun! You're literally bottling up your intentions for safekeeping. It's amazing to step back and watch them come true.

Another thing that's cool about spell jars is how you can hone your intuition. You will start to get an intuitive sense of which items to use and how they support you. If you've ever worked with crystals before, you already know what I'm talking about. This is a similar idea but spread to more items than just the crystals.

Spell jars are also a wonderful way to serve the earth. By setting intentions for your own peace and well-being, you are doing your part to raise the global vibe so we can all be benefited. You can also create spell jars to help others or even the whole planet. I do this sometimes, especially when I feel anxious about what's been happening on the news. It makes me feel good to know I can do my part, even if it's in a very small way. Spell jars utilize ingredients taken from nature, too, so it's a really good way to connect with Mother Earth.

One of my favorite benefits of spell jars, though, is how they enhance my creativity and personal empowerment. When I finish a spell jar, I just feel so...alive. It's hard to explain, but I feel like I've done something. Like I've really made a difference in my life. It's kind of an art form, and it stretches my mind and heart in all kinds of powerful ways.

Wise witches know their words create their worlds, after all. This is one of the biggest things I learned in my deep dive into all things witchy. It's really changed the way I talk, think, and act in this world. Like when I talked about the ethics of being a witch before, that's all part of my newfound sense of purpose here on this planet. I'm much more likely to think—and act—in positive ways now because I truly believe I can influence my world. I even believe more in my ability to control my own actions, which always felt so random and powerless in the past. And becoming a witch has been such a big part of that.

Even just the act of choosing an intention can be so powerful. And then, of course, you're selecting all these fabulous ingredients that just lend their power to a spell. And usually you wrap a spell up with an incantation of some kind, further utilizing your words to help something come true.

Remember, you can't force anything to come true that isn't right for you, others, or the planet. Nor should you, if you're practicing ethical witchcraft. Certainly, there are darker forms of witchcraft that you can learn about on your own time, but that's not why you're here right now.

Right now, you're here to learn how to encourage your wildest dreams to come true. You deserve all the best in life, and focusing on what is in the best interest of all is so meaningful. Spell jars are possibly my favorite way, so I'm so glad you're here, taking this journey with me.

As you can see, spell jars can be highly beneficial. By believing and focusing your intent, you hold a very real power over what happens to you. Most of us feel pretty out of control sometimes, but doing just one small thing (like putting some cool items in a jar) can work wonders, even if it's just on your own mindset. And if you expect magick to happen...believe me, it does!

## WHAT ARE SPELL JARS?

As you might imagine, there are many ways to use your innate witchy abilities to create all kinds of different spells. For instance, people use wands or ritual baths or magickal elixirs or recipes or chanting or so many other different spellcasting methods. All of them work, in that they all help support an intention and assist it in coming true.

There are so many ways to be a witch, and all of them are interesting and valid!

Still, spell jars are my favorite.

Also called "witch bottles," spell jars are a type of spell contained in...you guessed it...a jar. Or bottle. Or pill jar. Or empty makeup case. Or a pen or a teacup or a storage tote... or any kind of container, really. You can use your imagination here.

Basically, if it's a spell you keep in a jar (or jar-like object), you can call it a jar spell.

Witches have been using them for centuries, and they're so, so handy. They neatly contain the spell, are easy to carry, and honestly just look really, really nice. Like a work of art. You can bury them, keep them under your bed, carry them in a bag or purse, store them on a shelf, tuck them in your pocket, give them as gifts...the possibilities are endless.

Spell jars actually were less well known for a long time, but since witchcraft has become more in the open, they've become much more popular.

I first got into jar spells at that same festival I was telling you about, the one I went to with my friend Sebastian. We stopped at this amazing booth run by a powerful witch named Kelsey, who had all kinds of bottles and jars and other witchy paraphernalia.

Since I'm a crystal fanatic, Kelsey's spell jars immediately caught my undivided attention.

They were all lined up in neat little rows, each one glittering with a variety of different crystals, herbs, and objects. And they were sealed up so nicely that I instantly knew I would be buying one.

Kelsey noticed me looking, and the conversation that ensued was one I'll never forget.

Almost 45 minutes later, I left her shop with three spell jars, some herbal ingredients, and a book on spell jars. It was all money very well spent.

Typical of me, I left with more questions than I had answered, but also typical of me, I went home knowing I'd learn every piece of information I could get my hands on. It was an important day.

That first jar I noticed in her shop? It turned out to be a jar for sleep and anxiety. My intuition drew me right to it. Kelsey had a few similar jars in her shop, but that one really stood out to me. I knew it was calling me, and I just had to have it.

I also bought a writer's spell jar for clear communication and a productivity spell for my desk at work. And some beginner's ingredients to get me started. I knew I would be making my own spell jars as soon as I could!

## HOW DO I CHOOSE AN INTENTION?

As soon as I got home from the festival that day, I opened my new treasures and started thinking through all the possibilities. I already had a pretty good idea of some of the intentions I could set, and when I went to take a quick inventory of my crystal collection, I had lots more ideas come to my mind, too.

There are so many more intentions out there! The sky really is the limit here.

However, when you set an intention, you want to pick one that's at least semi-realistic for you. Like, we all would love to be able to fly without an airplane, but at least at this point in human history...it's not very realistic.

No, it's better to choose an intention that will be at least slightly easy for you to believe in. That's what helps it work.

That said, you also want to pick something a little *outside* the realms of possibility. Just enough that you're comfortable stretching a little. For instance, one of my first spell jars was about confidence as a writer. I picked that intention because I'd already written a few short stories and even a whole book...but I still struggled with the courage to write more. Or to publish. Or to tell my friends and family members "I'm a writer" instead of just saying, "I write a little...but it's not very good."

So I chose that one early on to help me write more confidently. In fact, it's right here on my desk as I type this! I look at it often, and I can really feel it supporting me.

Anyway, so you want to pick an intention that's a bit outside of your comfort zone, but not totally against the laws of physics.

You also want to pick something that matches your personal code of ethics. This will vary from witch to witch, but the general Wiccan code is "do no harm," as you already know. So whatever constitutes "no harm" to you, that's a pretty good place to start. It's more likely to come true that way, anyway.

After you create a jar spell, you will also want to take

some tangible actions in the world to help it come true, so choosing intentions with some kind of practical applications attached is always a good idea. Remembering, of course, that you can't *force* something to come through if it's simply not meant to be. That's the opposite of magick. Wise witches know that everything happens for a reason, and if it's meant to be it'll be. Still, it never hurts to help it along a little!

Once you've chosen your intention and created the spell, just know it with all your being. Take the actions, of course, but don't spend time worrying about whether it'll come true or not. If you know with every fiber of your being that your intention is already true on some level of reality, then it is true. Your magick is allowing it to manifest in *this* level of reality, the one you can see, smell, taste, and touch.

So set intentions that are 1) already true on some level of reality, 2) attainable, and 3) something you can believe in with all your heart.

For the spell I made for my mom, I had already spent some time thinking about *exactly* what I wanted the spell to do. My mom's surgery was supposed to be fairly minor, but I didn't want anything to go wrong, and I wanted her body to be strong enough to fight off any potential complications or infections. I chose the ingredients based on the knowledge I'll be teaching you in this book, so hang in there with me. For now, just know that every spell has carefully chosen ingredients, and all of them are important!

## CHAPTER 2
# EVERYTHING YOU NEED TO PREPARE YOUR SPELLS

### WHAT TOOLS OR EQUIPMENT DO I NEED TO CREATE MY OWN SPELL JARS?

Before we get any further on this spell jar journey, here's a shopping list for you. When I say "shopping" list, I also mean "found in an old cupboard" list or "in a box of hand-me-downs" list or "thrifted" list. In no way do you have to spend lots of money to fulfill all your wildest witchy spell jar dreams. It can be as basic as putting a few items in a jar and calling it good.

Still, if you want to put on your favorite mystical outfit and hit up your favorite local craft store for a few of these... it would be a fun afternoon. You're more than welcome to try this for yourself. Trust me, I can drop half a paycheck on these goodies if I'm not careful! So I set a witchcraft budget for myself. You know, all the essentials in life.

Anyway, wherever you get these items is fine. You'll probably find that once you start collecting them, the items will start to "find" you. Once I got into this stuff, I can't tell you the number of times people would come up to me and say, "Hey, I saved this nice empty bottle for you, do you want it?" Seriously, it happens all the time. So start your own small collection, stand back, and watch it grow.

I'll teach you how to use the items on the list, of course, but mostly I want you to see that no matter who you are, you can dive into all the sparkly, mystical goodness that is witchcraft, no matter how small your budget or how spare your free time. You don't even have to go to a fancy witchcraft school or drop a fortune on exotic ingredients. All you need is a few household items and your own innate magickal abilities.

Before I give you the list, please know that you do not need to have every item on here to get started making your own spell jars. This is just a general set of ingredients for the modern witch to be aware of when you start out. This book is not one of those medieval compendiums with the gold illuminated letters and the rustle-y pages. I kinda wish it was, but nope. Just a regular list for a regular witch like you and me. I've tried to include items that you can get for reasonable prices (or might already have in your cupboard). A witch has gotta eat, after all.

I've also tried to include items that you can reasonably get from a local herb store, in your back yard, or even at the grocery store. You can use your own common sense and intuition to substitute anything you can't find. Remember, it's about the intention of it, although having the right ingredients does help move that along.

And you need to know that this list is deliberately very, very long. You can use only a few items to get started and then increase your repertoire as you go. I mostly wanted you to have lots and lots of options in case you were struggling to find them all.

You'll also notice that this list has lots of crystals on it. I just really, really enjoy using crystals. If you don't have the ones on the list, you can find ones of a similar color. You can even just use rocks from outside, especially if you find ones in colors that mean something to you.

Also, I didn't include any ingredients that are considered toxic in any way. There are lots of herbs you can find that need to be used with great caution, as they can be harmful in large (or even small) doses. I only included ingredients that are generally safe, but always remember that if you have an allergy to anything, you obviously should avoid it! Use your best judgment and substitute anything you're not feeling. The spell will still work.

By the way, the witchy vocabulary word for "a list of ingredients and what they mean" is *grimoire*. I just love knowing this stuff. I also recommend getting a notebook or journal to write down the spells you create so you can have your own recipe spell book. This is totally optional, but I've found it really useful.

All right, enough chit-chat. Here's a list of suggested items for your spell jar arsenal.

## SPELLCASTING SUPPLIES

**For the jars themselves:**

- Plenty of glass jars, bottles, and other witchy containers (can be creative and use anything that has a space in which to place the ingredients)
- Candles, ribbon, string, or tape for sealing the jars (a variety of colors is best)
- Corks or lids to make sealing easier

## For setting up the jars:

- Matches or a lighter
- Incense (optional)
- Altar items (optional)
- Vibe-setting music (optional)

## Herbs & Plants

| | | | |
|---|---|---|---|
| Acorn | Cabbage | Coriander | Nutmeg |
| African violet | Cactus | Cumin | Oak |
| Alfalfa | Calendula | Dandelion | Onion |
| Allspice | Camellia | Dandelion Root | Orange |
| Almond | Camphor | Dill | Oregano |
| Aloe | Caraway | Echinacea | Palo Santo |
| Amaranth | Cardamom | Elder | Parsley |
| Angelica | Carnation | Evening Primrose | Passionflower |
| Anise | Carrot | Fennel | Plantain |
| Apple | Cascara Sagrada | Flax | Pumpkin |
| Apricot | Cashew | Garlic | Raspberry |
| Arrowroot | Castor | Ginger | Red Pepper |
| Aster | Cat Tail | Gum Arabic | Rose |
| Astragalus | Catnip | Hazel | Rosemary |
| Avocado | Cayenne | Heather | Sage |
| Bamboo | Cedar | Hibiscus | Sandalwood |
| Banana | Celery | Honeysuckle | Sesame |
| Barley | Chamomile | Horehound | St. John's Wort |
| Basil | Cherry | Horseradish | Strawberry |
| Bay | Chestnut | Ivy | Sunflower |

## YOUR FIRST SPELL JAR (AND 59 MORE...)

| Beans (various) | Chia | Lavender | Tarragon |
|---|---|---|---|
| Beet | Chickweed | Lemon | Thistle |
| Birch | Chicory | Lemon Balm | Thyme |
| Black Pepper | Chili Pepper | Lemongrass | Valerian |
| Blackberry | Chives | Licorice | Vanilla |
| Bladderwrack | Chrysanthemum | Lilac | Vetiver |
| Blueberry | Cilantro | Lily | Walnut |
| Brazil Nut | Cinnamon | Lime | Willow |
| Brewer's Yeast | Citronella | Mint | Yarrow |
| Buckeye | Clove | Mistletoe | Yellow Dock |
| Buckwheat | Clover | Mustard | |
| Burdock | Coffee | Nettle | |

## Crystals

| Agate | Citrine | Malachite | Turquoise |
|---|---|---|---|
| Amazonite | Clear Quartz | Moonstone | Ruby |
| Amber | Diamond | Obsidian | Topaz |
| Amethyst | Emerald | Onyx | Sapphire |
| Aquamarine | Fluorite | Opal | |
| Aventurine | Garnet | Pearl | |
| Azurite | Hematite | Peridot | |
| Beryl | Howlite | Pyrite | |
| Black Tourmaline | Jade | Rhodochrosite | |
| Bloodstone | Jasper | Rose Quartz | |
| Blue Lace Agate | Kyanite | Selenite | |
| Calcite | Lapis Lazuli | Shungite | |
| Carnelian | Lavastone | Sodalite | |
| Celestite | Lepidolite | Tiger's Eye | |

## Oils

| | | | |
|---|---|---|---|
| Bergamot | Mandarin | Myrrh | Spruce |
| Cedarwood | Melissa | Neroli | Sweet Orange |
| Cinnamon | Geranium | Niaouli | Tangerine |
| Clary Sage | Ginger | Palmarosa | Tea Tree |
| Clove | Grapefruit | Patchouli | Thyme |
| Cypress | Jasmine | Peppermint | Vanilla |
| Eucalyptus | Juniper Berry | Petitgrain | Vetiver |
| Fennel | Lavender | Rose | Ylang-ylang |
| Frankincense | Lemon | Rosemary | |
| Lime | Lemongrass | Sandalwood | |

## Various other things

| | | | |
|---|---|---|---|
| A Letter to Yourself | Feathers | Moss | Sesame seeds |
| Activated Charcoal | Flower Petals | Pebbles | Snakeskin |
| Ashes | Honey | Pinecones | String |
| Bark | Jewelry | Ribbon | Sugar |
| Beeswax | Leaves | Rice (various) | Sunflower Seeds |
| Coins | Licorice | Salt | Twigs |
| Dried fruit | Milk or Yogurt | Sand (various) | Vinegar |

As you can see, you probably have lots of these items in your own home already. Some you can probably find in your backyard or at a nearby greenspace. A few others you might need to find at a craft store, crystal shop, or herb store. Some you might even want to order online. All of them, though, are some of my go-to ingredients for spell jar casting.

Just so you know, it's totally okay to substitute anything

you see in this book for another ingredient that you feel drawn to. For instance, if you don't have fresh garlic and want to use powdered garlic instead, or if you're personally just not drawn to using something from outside...that's totally fine. Same thing goes for the plant or herb version versus the essential oil version. No matter what form the ingredient takes, it still carries the energy of that thing. Also, if you don't have something that's here or just want to try something else for the fun of it, go ahead. No judgments here.

A good thing to note is that rosemary is a safe substitute for almost *any* ingredient...within reason. You wouldn't want to use rosemary for *everything*, but it can come in handy if you need to make a spell jar quickly and don't have the right stuff. Just know that a spell using only rosemary won't be as powerful (unless your intention is a one-ingredient spell, of course). It would mostly just be a jar of rosemary. Clear quartz is another ingredient that I like to substitute a lot. It basically magnifies the other ingredients and is very versatile. Again, though, if you only use clear quartz...there's not much there to magnify. So do your best to creatively mix and match using what you have on hand, and don't be afraid to think like a resourceful witch.

## HOW DO I CHOOSE INGREDIENTS?

So now that you know how to choose some of the ingredients you might use, how do you know how to choose which ingredients to actually use? It can get overwhelming, for sure. Well, I'm providing a list of general intentions and the ingredients that go with them, to take the guesswork out of it. This is called a magical *correspondences* list, and I have also provided a longer glossary at the end of this book that includes every ingredient in this book next to its meanings, plus a few extra ingredients that you can use to substitute as well.

That said, intuition is a witch's *most* important tool. You will start to pick up on the different meanings of the different ingredients available, and you will also start to notice different ingredients "calling" to you. If you are ever creating a spell jar and you get the sudden urge to add in an extra teaspoon of this or a smidgeon of that...that's your intuition talking to you. It might also tell you to leave out some ingredients entirely or swap them for different ingredients. It might also say to you, when you see something in the store or in a cupboard or on the ground, "Hey, pick that up! It goes in a spell!" As you practice your intuition, it'll come through. Every time.

In fact, I recommend spending time getting used to listening to your body's intuitive hits more and more. That's been one of the biggest blessings of witchcraft for me —I'm a lot more in tune with my body and what it wants. For instance, I can now tell if a food isn't going to sit well with me before I eat it, rather than after. Before I was a witch, I would sometimes get an upset stomach (usually due to anxiety), and I wouldn't really know what caused it, although I would certainly know later on after the damage was done! Now I'm a lot more in tune with myself and my needs. When I look at a food, sometimes my body will whisper, "Nope, don't eat that. You will regret it." As I've learned to answer back, "Okay, I'm listening to you!" instead of, Nah, you're just being silly," when I get these intuitive downloads, they've gotten stronger and clearer.

Another example is learning to trust people. Everyone has an aura, and some people give off an aura of, well... creepiness. Or meanness. Or just plain not-niceness.

Again, before I was a witch, I used to just trust everyone and go along with what everyone said, and I often ended up getting hurt, believe it or not. So then I started not trusting anyone at all, ever, which wasn't good, either. It was honestly just a mess.

Now that I've learned to use my intuition, though, I'll start to notice things about them as soon as I meet them, and sometimes the answer is, "They're safe—be their friend!" and sometimes the answer is, "They're not safe—be polite but don't get too close," or even, "Danger! Avoid at all costs!"

This is useful. And if you're reading this book, the chances are good that you have a strong intuition. Most witches are drawn to the craft because they have natural intuitive gifts. This is you, most likely.

Even the least naturally intuitive person, though, can still learn to use this skill. Everyone has it! It just can take a little practice. And some people have been "trained out" of their intuition if they were raised in a culture or in a family that did not honor intuition. It's sometimes hard to trust your gut, after all. But it's an essential skill of witchcraft. It took me a while, but as I gained confidence, my intuition started to grow. I wouldn't say my intuition is perfect now, but it's a far sight from where it was before! And it's a huge blessing to be able to tap into this gift.

So as you begin to select ingredients for your jar spells, start to tune in to your intuition. If something "feels good" or "seems right," it probably is! Over time, this will get easier and more accurate. Just be patient and practice. If you're already an intuitive guru, go crazy! No need to follow my recipes, if your intuition tells you another way.

That said, I'm definitely going to give you some recipes to get you started. We'll get there soon. In the meantime, here's a general correspondences chart to show you the general types of ingredients for a variety of different meanings. If you're sensing that an ingredient works for you in a different way than I have listed here, no worries. It probably just has a different meaning for you based on your unique history and life experience. And that's totally okay. Just be mindful that the whole spell should have harmony in the different elements.

What I mean by harmony is that you don't want to choose totally at random or throw in items willy-nilly. The whole point of a spell is to maximize the energies of each item by combining them together. You can be creative with the combinations, of course, but they all must be done mindfully and with intent. This is why recipes are great to start off. In fact, I used recipes exclusively for the first several months of being a witch. After a few months, I started to gain confidence and courage to tweak or substitute the recipes I was using. Your journey might be faster or slower, of course! There's no "right" speed for learning to be a witch.

This is why it's so helpful to have a mentor. Books like this one, blogs, articles, videos, and all other sorts of resources are really helpful when you're just starting out. Eventually you'll be your own expert! In the meantime, though, here are just some of the common correspondences for spell jar ingredients and their meanings. There's a longer list in the glossary at the end of this book. We'll get to the recipes soon, I promise.

## YOUR FIRST SPELL JAR (AND 59 MORE...)

| Meanings | Ingredients |
|---|---|
| Abundance | Acorns, allspice, almonds, cloves, oak leaves, oats, poppy seeds, rice, saffron, sage, cinnamon, aventurine, bloodstone, emerald, jade, peridot, pyrite, ruby, coins, money, checks, ginger, grapefruit, patchouli, myrrh, frankincense, mint, nutmeg |
| Achievement | Orange, lemon, lime, patchouli, sandalwood, tiger's eye, citrine, blue lace agate |
| Communication | Basil, cilantro, fennel, aquamarine, sodalite, selenite, mint, parsley, amazonite, howlite, lapis lazuli, turquoise, pearl, feathers, water |
| Courage | Allspice, cayenne, fennel, mustard, thyme, yarrow, agate, azurite, beryl, onyx, tiger's eye, clove, ginger |
| Friendship | Sunflower, honeysuckle, rose, pearl, garnet, beryl |
| Healing | Caraway, eucalyptus, ginger, thyme, cedar, dill, fennel, rosemary, vinegar, salt, coriander, dill, amber |
| Love | Rose, ylang-ylang, jasmine, pearl, lavender, moonstone, patchouli, bergamot, comfrey, apple, apricot, avocado, caraway, carnation, cinnamon, clover, cumin, mistletoe, orange, strawberry |
| Luck | Bay, cumin, dill, nutmeg, vanilla, cinnamon, garnet, bamboo, buckeye, cabbage, garlic, hazel, lilac |
| Protection | Thyme, bay, sage, salt, garnet, basil, peppermint, labradorite, pins, needles, thistles, nails, tacks, black pepper, black beans, lavastone, hematite, cedar, lemon, selenite |
| Sleep | Lavender, chamomile, passionflower, valerian, lemon balm, amethyst, clear quartz, moonstone, selenite, lepidolite |
| Strength | Tiger's eye, citrine, lemon, orange, black tourmaline, hematite, onyx, yarrow, pyrite |
| Happiness | Cedar, lemon, orange, grapefruit, cinnamon, basil, catnip, lemongrass, rosemary, violet, allspice |

And so on, and so forth. This is merely a short list. You might want to start keeping a notebook of all the ingredients you like to use and their meanings. It's really useful for looking up later.

Trust me, we will start putting these ingredients into jars soon! Meanwhile, let's take a moment to talk about candles. Candles, as you've already seen, are a big part of witchcraft. Every witch I know loves candles, and I see why! Not only are they lovely for cleansing a space, they also just look really nice. And they're crucial as part of a spell jar ritual. We will talk more about candles soon, but for right now, let's talk about some of the colors you can choose for candles and what they mean.

Colors, in general, have lots of important meanings. As you start to work with spell jars, you'll notice that certain colors mean certain things, from the crystals you put in the jar to the candle you use to seal it. So learning some basic magickal color theory is essential here.

**Magickal Meanings of Colors:**

- White: Purification, healing, serenity
- Gold: Abundance, luck
- Silver: Purity, serenity
- Yellow: Positivity, good luck, friendship, abundance
- Orange: Friendship, courage, success, creativity, positivity, growth
- Green: Healing, money, growth
- Blue: Calm, communication, emotions, healing
- Purple: Spirituality, enlightenment, intuition, insight, knowing
- Pink: Love, friendship, healing
- Red: Love, grounding, passion
- Brown: Grounding, justice, balance, health, resources
- Black: Protection, releasing, grounding
- Gray: Calm, balance, healing

If you don't have these colors or want to substitute,

that's fine, but if in doubt, you're generally better substituting a plain white or a neutral wax candle. If your candles are scented, you want to make sure the scent matches the energy you are trying to bring about, too. Harmony among the elements in a spell is essential to amplify its power.

## WHEN IS THE BEST TIME TO CAST A JAR SPELL?

The best time to create a jar spell is when you are in need of it. When you are ready to cast the spell, go for it.

That said, there are certain times of the day, week, month, and year that are more powerful for casting spells than others. I've noticed that when I'm mindful of when I cast a spell, the better it works, because I'm harnessing the powerful energy that's already available in the stars and planets.

For instance, the easiest way to do this is to cast a spell on the new moon, then wait for the full moon to see what manifests for you. As the moon waxes toward full, you will notice all sorts of miracles as it comes true. Then at the full moon, you can decide whether to keep that jar spell or start over with a new one. This is by far the simplest way and works especially well with money and abundance spells.

Naturally, though, there are so many other ways you can harness time to be on your side. Here are some of the common days and times you can use to your advantage, as well as what they mean for spellcasting. All you've got to do is find the kind of intention you want to set, then plan to create that jar spell on a day or time that matches. This will boost the power of the spell.

*Days of the Week for Spellcasting:*

- **Monday:** Intuition, dreaming, peace, femininity, justice, balance, harmony
- **Tuesday:** Courage, confidence, success, overcoming, accomplishment, strength
- **Wednesday:** Communication, wisdom, healing, creativity, music, education
- **Thursday:** Abundance, travel, healing, loyalty, prosperity, honor
- **Friday:** Relationships, love, friendship, romance, support, harmony, grace, balance
- **Saturday:** Protection, hard work, discipline
- **Sunday:** Success, fame, spirituality, healing, miracles

So if you're wondering which day this week to start casting jar spells, this probably gives you an idea! Depending on what day it is today, actually, you might already know when to cast your first spell.

You can also watch the moon phases. In fact, most witches are guided by the moon, as her feminine energy is so powerful for manifesting your dreams.

*Moon Phases for Spellcasting:*

- **New moon:** Abundance, new ventures, starting a new relationship, re-birth, transformation, healing, releasing old patterns
- **Waxing crescent moon:** Growth, courage, success, gaining momentum, achievements, building, new endeavors

# YOUR FIRST SPELL JAR (AND 59 MORE...)

- **First quarter moon:** Taking action, drive, forward motion, self-esteem, confidence, communication, growth, decision-making, releasing resistance
- **Gibbous moon:** Overcoming challenges, acceptance, healing, flexibility, perseverance, openness
- **Full moon:** Stability, acceptance, receiving, self-love, miracles, relationships, commitment, strength, power, prophecy, spiritual gifts, energy, achievement
- **Disseminating moon:** Understanding, wisdom, releasing the old, moving forward, acceptance, letting go of the past, healing
- **Last quarter moon:** Harmony, balance, understanding, forgiveness, banishing negativity, healing, letting go of the past
- **Balsamic moon:** Releasing, detoxing, de-cluttering, cleansing, spiritual gifts, wisdom, knowledge, visions, dreams

It's especially useful to create a spell jar during a specific moon phase and then just be mindful over the next few moon phases to see what shows up.

For instance, you could create an abundance spell jar on the new moon, and then allow a few weeks for the full moon to roll around just to see what money miracles show up in your life. The full moon tends to highlight whatever is most intense at the moment, so setting an intention for money to be the most intense thing is a really, really good idea if more money is what you want! You can of course do the same thing with relationships, health, friendship, a new job, whatever. That's just one of my favorite examples.

Obviously, since witches know everything is connected, paying attention to the moon phases is crucial. You should note that there are certain times when the moon is "void," of course. This is the point between moon phases, when the moon is between different stages. You should do your best not to cast any spells during this time, as they will either be less effective...or sometimes disastrous. Witchcraft experts disagree on how bad this actually can be, but it's still always a good idea to check the moon phase before casting a spell, regardless. It's always better to let the moon work *for* you, rather than against you.

You can also pay attention to the stars and planets, though, as the zodiac signs are also great ways to work with magick. The basic properties of each zodiac sign can be extremely powerful for casting spells at different times, as can knowing the influence of the various planets. There's too much to really go into in this book, so I'll keep it brief, but here's a very, very short version of how you can use the zodiac signs to enhance your magick practice.

### *Zodiac Signs for Spellcasting:*

- **Aries:** Power, authority, leadership, willpower, new beginnings, challenges, protection
- **Taurus:** Stability, health, support, family, abundance, success, career, money
- **Gemini:** Communication, connection, friendship, travel, knowledge, education, imagination
- **Cancer:** Home, family, gratitude, comfort, abundance, luck, cleansing
- **Leo:** Courage, creativity, performance, public speaking, fertility, healing, success, influence

- **Virgo:** Planning, organization, career, productivity, motivation, focus
- **Libra:** Creativity, spiritual gifts, truth, justice balance, new ideas
- **Scorpio:** Luck, psychic abilities, mental health, emotional healing, cleansing, healing the past
- **Sagittarius:** Travel, productivity, growth, healing, success, accomplishments, achievement
- **Capricorn:** New endeavors, organization, productivity, de-cluttering, ambition, strength
- **Aquarius:** Intuition, inner knowing, spirituality, inspiration, innovation, clarity, solutions
- **Pisces:** Visions, dreams, imagination, spiritual gifts, creativity, future goals, hope

Casting a jar spell during these times can be especially helpful, so spend some time familiarizing yourself with these if you want to go that deep. Lots of witches love being in tune with the astrological seasons, so that's a great option for you to add to your practice.

And, of course, you can literally look at the seasons of the year! Winter is a wonderful time for detoxing, resetting, and sending down deep roots. So any spells for grounding, de-cluttering, reflection, observation, and healing the past are great during the wintertime. Springtime is great for growth, new beginnings, healing, and starting fresh. You can absolutely cast spells for hope, courage, friendship, accomplishment, innovation, creativity, and other related ideas during the spring. Summertime is known as a time of travel, joy, connecting with others, abundance, and putting yourself out there. Any spells that resonate with these ideas will be perfect in summer. And of course, fall is the time of harvest, so any spells for raking in all the blessings are great in the fall! It's also a great time for transformation and transition.

More specifically, witches have traditionally watched the seasons coming and going in the solstices and equinoxes of the year, when the sun reaches its various zeniths. For Wiccans, this is a sacred duty to honor the Wheel of the Year. For me, it's a great way to make my spell jars more intentional, as casting them on these days can be much more powerful. Honestly, just about any spell can be cast on these days, although there are certain topics that are more powerful at certain times. Here are just a few of the times of the year you can start to pay attention to as well:

### Solstices and Equinoxes for Spellcasting

- **Vernal Equinox:** New beginnings, fertility, love, family, home
- **Summer Solstice:** Weddings, contracts, fertility, energy
- **Autumnal Equinox:** Endings, harvest, contracts
- **Winter Solstice:** Family connections, new beginnings, home and hearth

And last but certainly not least, you can utilize the various times of day to your advantage in choosing when to create a spell jar. Casting a spell at times like sunrise, sunset, noon, and midnight will be more powerful. Casting a spell for growth and increasing more of what you want are better during times when the hands of the clock are pointing upward or growing, and spells for decreasing what you don't want are better when the hands are pointing downward or diminishing.

In the end, you should cast spells whenever you feel you need them. But it's really handy to know about how to make them more powerful, and all these tips have been really useful for me, personally. It helps to get into a rhythm with your year, for so many reasons. The entire universe is conspiring to make your life better, so working *with* the various elements (instead of against them) is just plain common sense.

## CHAPTER 3
# CASTING YOUR FIRST SPELL

WHAT DO I DO BEFORE CASTING A JAR SPELL?

All right, now that you've got some ingredients and some general know-how, it's time to get started on the spells!

I remember the first time I cast a spell. I was nervous, but I took a deep breath...and went for it. It paid off in the end. But it took me several tries to get confident. In fact, I still struggle with confidence from time to time. It's totally normal.

This is why you want to make sure you're prepared before casting a spell. Most of the things I'm going to teach you in this section are optional—they're just highly recommended. It's crucial as a witch to practice safe, grounded spell-casting so you keep your intention pure and the magic clean from contaminating forces.

What do I mean about contaminating forces? I mean anything and everything in the universe that might get in the way of your desired outcome. So fear, stress, worry, energetic baggage, opposing entities...anything. We want to prepare our space and ourselves before getting started so that stuff is minimized (or even eliminated).

Honestly, the biggest thing I've learned about dealing with all the negative side of the universe is actually just to not pay it any attention. By focusing on your desired intentions, you're automatically keeping the more negative forces at bay. In fact, nothing is truly "negative" if it provides a life lesson or opportunity for growth.

That said, part of casting a spell jar is overcoming that stuff! So you want to clear yourself and your space before beginning.

Before you start, though, you want to go ahead and have your spell ingredients ready for your chosen intention. Have everything you need on hand, because as soon as you clear your space, you want to go ahead and fill the jar. And I mean, have everything literally sitting in front of you, not in the next room somewhere. You wouldn't want to cleanse your space and then run to the cupboard for a spice you forgot. So be sure your ingredients, your jars, and your sealing materials are all ready and waiting for you before you start to cleanse the space. Then as soon as the space is ready, you can start right into the jar-filling process.

When you've got everything assembled, you're ready to cleanse your space. Some of the techniques I'm about to teach you apply to general magick practices, also. Some apply to just jar spells, though. It's a good rule of thumb to practice safe magick, so that's why we always start with cleansing our space.

First, you'll want to physically cleanse your space of any clutter and then sweep out any dust or dirt. Lots of witches have a special dedicated broom for this (called a *besom* broom), but you don't necessarily need one (unless you especially want one, of course!). Cleansing the area physically is the first step, and it's very important to do this before every spell you cast.

You know how you feel kinda icky after you've had the flu? And it feels so good to take a shower and wash off all the ick?

Or you know how it gets all hot and dusty in the summer (if you live in a place that gets hot, of course), and a nice rain comes along and the dust settles and everything feels clean and new again?

Or like, do you ever get that urge in the spring to clean your whole house, buy some new décor, and maybe even get a new 'do?

This is what you want to do before programming an intention into a spell bottle. You want to make sure all the "old" is cleared away so you're working with a clean slate, energetically speaking. Physically cleaning your space is the best way to start.

To do this, I take my special spellcasting broom (although you can use any broom you have if you don't have your own spellcasting broom yet) and carefully sweep the area I'm going to be sitting in to make my jar. I try to get the corners and all the nooks and crannies. Sometimes I dust all the windowsills, too, and wipe off the table. This is more for my own state of mind than the spell, though. Honestly, my house is way cleaner now that I do witchcraft...a side bonus that I mention to my husband at every opportunity!

All jokes aside, it's so motivating to be a witch. It really does make me feel empowered. And yes, I clean my house more now. I just like feeling good. I used to have all kinds of issues around cleaning due to my anxiety. Before, I would stress about cleaning because if I couldn't do it perfectly, I wouldn't do it at all. Now I know that cleaning my home physically is also an energetic cleanse that really supports me and my alignment. It's not a perfect system, but yes, my motivation is a lot better now that I am a witch. And not just for cleaning! All kinds of things have gotten easier for me, like work, relationships, even having fun.

I want to make it very clear: I'm not saying you need to have a spotless house to do a spell. Just take a few quick moments to prepare your space before you start. And just notice how you start to feel when you do this. Wise witches know that to show love to the environment you live in is to show love to yourself.

Anyway, back to the cleansing. Sweep that area. Clean it out as much as you feel you can. If it feels good at this point, you can go ahead and start your spell jar. However, it can't hurt to do just a little more. I also like to also smoke cleanse (also sometimes called "smudging") after I sweep my area but before I begin the spell.

You can do this with incense, sage, palo santo, or another smoke cleansing method. Simply light the end of your smudging material with a match or lighter and allow it to quickly burn out. You don't want an open flame, just a little glowing end that gives off a little smoke. Then carry (or wave) the smudge throughout the area you'll be using so the smoke can waft over the space. Make sure to get any random corners or high traffic areas. Do this for a few minutes or until you feel an energetic release.

How do you know when you've cleansed enough? If you're not very in tune to energy, just smudge until you you've covered the whole area. If you find your mind is wandering and your room is full of smoke, you've done plenty—probably too much! It's more about the intention than anything else. As with most things, it's about quality, rather than quantity, so a little smoke goes a long way.

You can also cleanse your space with sound. If you have a gong, singing bowl (brass or crystal varieties), set of chimes, a bronze bell, or anything like this, you can actually use sound to cleanse your space as well. I sometimes add this as a third layer of cleansing, just for a little extra if I'm feeling off or really want the added boost. It makes me feel good, too, on top of cleansing the space.

To cleanse with sound, walk around the room ringing your instrument or simply hit it once and let the vibrations handle the whole area.

For general cleansing, I have a little bell that I ring three times in a row, often several times a day. This gives me an instant energetic lift. It's great for before casting a spell jar, of course, but it's excellent any time of the day or night, too.

Lighting candles has a similar effect, so I always like to light a few before I get started. Sometimes I arrange the candles around the area I'm working in as an added protective layer. In general, I just love candles—they have such a witchy vibe! And they have the added bonus of keeping my house energetically clear.

Using candles as often as practical (while observing safe candle burning guidelines, of course) is a wonderful witchy practice. There are so many candles you can find online or in shops, and of course the more natural, vegan, and/or cruelty-free your candle is, the better it is for energetic cleansing. No need to get too uptight about this; just do the best you can and have fun with the candles that call to you.

Again, I just gave you a ton of things to do, so if it's too much, just pick one and use that as your cleansing ritual before getting started. It's more about your mindset than anything else. I usually put on some soft healing-type music while doing setting up a spell. It helps keep me focused in case of any distractions.

Before beginning the actual spell, you can also choose to cast a spell circle. Again, this is technically optional...but I highly recommend it. Casting a circle adds an additional layer of protection so that everything in your spell is pure and clean and exactly what you want it to be. You don't want outside energy accidentally getting in there. That would contaminate the spell.

That said, lots of people don't use circles, and I don't even use one every time. Use your intuition to decide what works best for you and how it fits into your spell casting practice. If you are more of a Wiccan witch, a spell circle will probably be in more alignment with you. In fact, there are tons of prayers and incantations you can use to do this, if you're into that sort of thing. If you're more of a general witch, maybe not. Either is fine; the choice is yours. Follow your own guidance on this and skip this next part for now if you're not feeling it!

If you decide to cast a circle, though, there are a few ways to do it. My favorite way is to draw a circle with my intention, but there are a variety of ways to do so. If you want to do it with your intention, you can imagine a glowing circle of white, healing light surrounding your area and keeping you safe while you create the spell. Or if you don't like white, pick another color.

To do this:

- Sit calmly and quietly for a moment, focusing on your breath.

- Imagine a glowing circle surrounding you and the space you will use to create your jar. A few feet in every direction is fine.
- Now *intend*—or know in your heart and mind—that this circle of light will protect you until you break it. It's there, even when you're not actively focused on it.
- Begin your spell jar as normal, and when you're done, you can release the circle, allowing it to dissipate.

That's it! This is the method I use most often, as it really helps ground and center me before starting the spell. It helps me believe, deep down, that my spell will work and that my intention is already true on some level of reality.

You can also cast the circle with a wand, if you have one. Or anything to mark the circle, really. Like crystals. Or herbs. An *athame* (or ritual knife) or a ward are others options if you have either of those. Or you can literally just use your hand.

Another way to cast a circle is by drawing it with salt or chalk, although this might be a lot to start out with, especially if you don't have access to salt or chalk or are practicing in an area with carpet (you certainly wouldn't want to get salt or chalk all over the rug if that's the only space you have).

If you're casting a circle with salt or chalk, though, here's what you do. Start by marking the four cardinal points in your room: north, south, east, and west. If you don't know what direction you're facing, most smartphones have a compass on them! I learned that early on in my spellcasting career, although I'd hardly paid attention to north and south before.

Once the four cardinal points are marked, you are ready to start casting. Center yourself and call upon the four corners, perhaps invoking your favorite deities or spiritual guides. North, south, east, and west are deities in their own right in many traditions, or you can do some research on the specific figures you want to invoke. Wiccans generally believe in a variety of them, but you can leave this part out if you're more of a general witch.

For maximum effect, make sure any guides or deities you call upon are all supportive and positive ones, highly aligned with your needs and goals. The whole point of a circle is to invite in more of what you want, so keeping it high vibe will be most effective, generally speaking.

To actually cast the spell circle, you will be drawing a circle using the cardinal points as an outline and then casting your actual spell in the middle. So gently pour your salt, or draw with your chalk, or wave your wand, or lay out your crystals, or whatever you are using for the circle in a nice, neat, even circle starting with the northernmost point. Then move around to the east, south, and west, finishing up the circle at the top in the north again (so you'll be moving in a clockwise direction). You might choose to recite an incantation out loud or in your mind while doing this, perhaps calling on your chosen deity for each cardinal point.

Once you're back at north, your circle is done! You can go ahead and create your spell jar in the center of the circle.

After you're done with your spell jar, you'll un-do the circle by moving backwards from how you started, removing the salt or chalk or rocks or whatever you used, or simply drawing it with your tool or hand. So counterclockwise, starting with north, moving to the west, then the south...etc.

There you go! If your circle is drawn (or you're skipping that part), you're ready to actually assemble the spell jar.

## HOW DO I CAST A JAR SPELL?

Once you have your space prepared, you're ready to start the spellcasting process. Since you've already got all your stuff laid out, you're ready to go. For me, this is the most exciting part. It's highly meditative. As I place everything in the jar, one by one, it always feels so soothing and powerful, like I'm actually doing something to change my life.

Like everything else in this book, I'm going to teach you by showing you. Remember that spell I mentioned in the beginning of this book, the one for my mom's surgery?

It was very simple. And it'll be easier for me to teach you by showing you how I did it.

So, here we go: Spell Jar #1. Here is how I created it:

I had already chosen my intention, which I shared with you before. After deciding to actually make the spell and give it to Mom, I started by gathering all the ingredients I knew I would need. Then I went to the space I usually use for prepping spell jars and swept the area with my special spell-casting broom, burned some incense, and took a moment to mentally center myself (which I explained how to do in the previous section). I called on my guides for added strength and protection as I created the spell.

Right before starting the actual spell, I lit the candle I had chosen for this particular recipe (white, for purity and healing). I lit the candle early so it would be partly melted by the time I was ready for it.

Then I cast a circle and started my jar! I had a special one already picked out, cleaned, and ready to go. It was a small one, so that it would be easy for her to take with her in her hospital bag. I added in the ingredients one by one, moving slowly and meditatively and keeping my intention in mind the whole time. This is my favorite part of every spell jar!

When the jar was full, I used a cork to stopper the bottle, wrapped and tied a green ribbon around the top, then allowed some of the white wax to drip all over the top and down the sides. I always make sure the bottle is fully sealed when making any spell jar. This step actually takes some practice to get right, so be patient—and careful—when using hot wax. In fact, hot wax is optional. If you want to simply place the cork in the bottle and call it good, that is totally fine. That's what I did for that first jar spell I made, actually, and it worked just the same as any other way to seal it. The wax gives it a nicer seal for a long-term spell, though, and it looks really pretty when it's all said and done.

Lastly, I held the bottle in my two hands and spent a moment focusing on my intention of healing for Mom's surgery. I said the incantation I had written to go with it aloud, feeling that when I said the words it was coming true already. Then I mentally released the circle I had cast.

That's it! After that, I kept the jar in a safe place until I could get to Mom's for brunch the next Sunday. This particular jar was meant to last until the surgery was over and Mom had made a full recovery, so I let her know she could throw it away (or give it back to me) after she felt better. I'll talk more about disposing of old spell jars later.

And now that I've shown you how to use a spell jar recipe, here is your very first one:

## SPELL JAR #1: A BLESSING FOR HEALING AND SPEEDY RECOVERY

*A recipe for healing quickly and painlessly, created for my mom's routine surgery.*

After cleansing your space, casting a spell circle if desired, and calling on any guides or intentions you feel drawn to, light a white spell candle with a match or lighter.

Then put the following ingredients in your jar (remember, feel free to substitute any of these or leave out any that you can't find or if the bottle is too small):

- Coarse sea salt (you can substitute table salt, Epsom salt, or pink Himalayan salt)
- Rosemary, dill, fennel, OR thyme
- Sage, ginger, OR clove
- Pine, cedar, OR juniper needles
- Coriander, dill, OR fennel
- Malachite, emerald, OR similar
- Selenite, calcite, OR clear quartz
- A Band-Aid, piece of white cloth, or other "healing" totem of your choice
- Green ribbon and white candle for sealing

Seal the bottle with a stopper if desired, then cover the seal with white wax and green ribbon. Hold the bottle in your hands for a few moments, feeling the energy. If you choose, recite (out loud or in your mind) something like this:

*Mom's surgery went perfectly*
*All is well*
*I seal this jar and it is so!*

Obviously, you should put the name of the person you are giving the jar to in there instead of my mom's name. And change it up if they're not having a surgery. You can just say "procedure" if you're not sure what it is, or "delivery" if they're having a baby. Whatever. Just making it very clear what you're talking about will be enough. After that, your jar is ready to give away!

See? You're almost ready to create your own spell jars now. Just a few more things to note, and then you'll be making your own spell jars like a pro.

**Where do I keep the jar?**

Once you've created your jar spell, you'll want to store it some place intentional. If it's a sleeping spell, the obvious place is to put it underneath your bed or perhaps on your bedside table. If it has to do with working out, keep it in your gym bag. If it's for your job, keep it in your desk at work. If it's to help you feel confident on a date, keep it in your purse. If it's for your car, keep it in your glove box. You get the idea.

Historically, witches often buried spell jars at a crossroads or on the border between people's lands. This may or may not be practical for you, but feel free to do so if you're feeling it. Burying the jar is especially helpful for protection spells and banishing spells.

Spell jars are honestly so pretty to look at that I enjoy keeping them on my desk. Or on my shelf. Or near my crystals. Or on my kitchen counter. Basically...everywhere in my entire home. And at my job.

So keep the spell jar where it'll be most meaningful to you. And where it'll stay safe and not get broken. If you have naysayers in your life, it may be best to keep the jar where no one can see it. Other people's opinions won't necessarily diminish the spell's power...but it might diminish your belief in it. Make that choice for yourself, but the back of your closet is always a safe bet if you think this will be an issue. Your intuition will help you with this. If your intuition tells you to keep your jar in a place that might seem strange, just go with it. As long as it's safe and intact, it should be okay.

**How do I break or end a jar spell?**

You might have noticed that lots of the ingredients we've discussed are perishable goods. As in, they won't keep indefinitely. If you're wanting to keep your spell jar for a long time, be mindful of the ingredients and maybe choose to leave the wet ingredients out. That way, the dry ingredients sealed in the jar will stay good for a long time. Otherwise...they may start to rot. Gross.

If you're planning to bury the spell jar, though, this probably doesn't matter too much.

Or, if you just want to keep it for a few days and then throw it away, maybe that's just fine as well. Your intuition and your common sense will tell you how long to keep it, as you consider what's in it and what it is meant to do.

Think about this as you're selecting ingredients. Remember, you can always substitute or leave something out.

You should leave the ingredients in the jar for as long as the spell's intention lasts. Maybe you notice after a few weeks that the spell jar has done its job. Great. Or maybe you notice that it's no longer working, your intention has shifted slightly, or you need a more powerful spell for some reason. All of these are potential reasons to un-do a jar spell. Sometimes we even realize that a spell is working too well, and we probably should have used a slightly different intention. Oops. Definitely take apart any spells that fall in this category!

If you toss it in the trash as is, it might still be in operation. It might not be working as well, though, or it might even start to work weird magick once it's thrown out. It's better to, at the very least, take the stopper out and disassemble the major ingredients. Use your best judgment here. If the inside is extremely gross, basically rotten, and several years old…it's probably safe just to toss the whole thing. That happened to me once with a jar I hid in my closet and forgot about. My bad.

Apparently, they've found witch bottles out there that have remained buried—literally—for several centuries. The ingredients from those are pretty far gone, I would imagine. I'm glad the jar in my closet didn't get that far.

Anyway, once the jar reaches a point where you no longer need it, you can either dis-assemble the jar and re-use the ingredients (if they're still salvageable) or you can just toss the whole thing into the trash. Remember an ethical witch knows that everything is connected, so use as much recycling and sustainable composting as possible. If you can't save everything, though…the trash is probably the best place for an old spell.

That said, make sure you break the spell in some way if you don't want it to be active any more.

For example, with the spell I made for my mom, I waited a few days after her surgery was over and she was pretty much recovered. I then unsealed the jar, took out the ingredients, and saved the crystals for re-use (cleansing them first, of course!). I composted and threw away the other ingredients and washed the jar really well. After that, it was ready for a new spell!

Ultimately you will know best when it is time to discard a spell. Just use your best judgment and remember that most spells will keep working until they've fulfilled their intent. Sometimes I forget where I've put a spell and then stumble on it by accident. When this happens, it's probably okay…just be mindful of the intentions you leave lying around.

**How do I create my own spells?**

By now, you have a pretty solid idea of which ingredients go with which intentions. As you read the recipes in the next section, you'll get an even better idea. When you get more advanced, though, you might be ready to start creating your own recipes, either by substituting ingredients into already written recipes or by starting from scratch.

As you do this, you'll want to make sure each spell includes a base (such as salt, rocks, grains, or similar), a layer with your crystals, herbs, and other items, and then top the whole jar with your liquid items (such as oils, honey, etc.). And then, of course, you'll want to indicate any other details, such as the colors for the candles or the incantations you use when casting the spell. Following the guidance you receive from practiced witches and your own intuition will help immensely with this. Once I started writing my own recipes, I was surprised at how much I had learned! You'll get the hang of it.

But if you're not at that place yet, don't worry. I'm here

## YOUR FIRST SPELL JAR (AND 59 MORE...)

to help! As promised, in the next chapter, you'll find 59 jar spell recipes to help you get started!

Remember that you can substitute if you need to. I've provided several options for each item in case you don't have everything on the list. Use your intuition and have fun!

## CHAPTER 4
# LOVE AND FRIENDSHIP SPELLS

### SPELL JAR RECIPE #2: ATTRACT A LOVING RELATIONSHIP

*A recipe for helping you find the one you love*

After cleansing your space, casting a spell circle if desired, and calling on any guides or intentions you feel drawn to, light a red spell candle with a match or lighter.

Then put the following ingredients in your jar:

- Pink salt (can substitute white or gray salt if need be)
- Rose quartz, ruby, OR garnet
- Apricots, strawberries, OR avocado
- Clover, honeysuckle, OR chamomile
- Rose, lavender, OR carnation petals
- Cinnamon, cardamom, OR cumin
- Lemon balm, licorice, OR rosemary
- Geranium, jasmine, OR ylang-ylang oil
- Honey, sugar, OR maple syrup

- A piece of paper with your ideal qualities in a mate written on it
- Red ribbon and red candle for sealing

Seal the bottle with a stopper if desired, then cover the seal with red wax and red ribbon. Hold the bottle in your hands for a few moments, feeling the energy. If you choose, recite (out loud or in your mind) something like this:

*I am love, loving, and lovable*
*My love is mine and I am my love's*
*And so it is*

Leave this spell somewhere near your bed and spend time focusing on manifesting the right person for you!

## SPELL JAR RECIPE #3: SELF-LOVE

*A recipe for showing yourself more compassion*

After cleansing your space, casting a spell circle if desired, and calling on any guides or intentions you feel drawn to, light a pink or red spell candle with a match or lighter.

Then put the following ingredients in your jar:

- Pink salt (can substitute white or gray salt if need be)
- Emerald, amethyst, OR rose quartz
- Chicory, thyme, OR chamomile
- Lavender, violet, OR rose petals
- Cinnamon, cardamom, OR cumin
- Honey, sugar, OR maple syrup
- A piece of paper with self-love affirmations written on it

- Red or pink ribbon and red or pink candle for sealing

Seal the bottle with a stopper if desired, then cover the seal with red or pink wax and red or pink ribbon. Hold the bottle in your hands for a few moments, feeling the energy. If you choose, recite (out loud or in your mind) something like this:

*Holding gratitude for myself and all I am*
*Yesterday, today, tomorrow, and forever*
*Thank you, thank you, thank you*

You might choose to spend some time journaling, taking a relaxing bath, or pampering yourself in some way after creating this jar. Spend the next few days and weeks giving yourself extra love and compassion.

## SPELL JAR RECIPE #4: ATTRACT FRIENDSHIP

*A recipe for connecting with more friends or deepening the friendships you already have*

After cleansing your space, casting a spell circle if desired, and calling on any guides or intentions you feel drawn to, light a yellow spell candle with a match or lighter.

Then put the following ingredients in your jar:

- Sugar (white or brown)
- Garnet, peridot, OR rhodochrosite
- Hibiscus, passionflower, OR honeysuckle
- Apple, apricot, OR grapefruit
- Lemon, orange, OR lime peel
- Red OR pink pepper
- Honey, sugar, OR maple syrup

- A list of some of your best friends (or qualities you'd like in a friendship)
- Yellow ribbon and yellow candle for sealing

Seal the bottle with a stopper if desired, then cover the seal with yellow wax and yellow ribbon. Hold the bottle in your hands for a few moments, feeling the energy. If you choose, recite (out loud or in your mind) something like this:

*The world is full*
*Of people like me*
*I am a friend of the world*
*And it is a friend of me*

After placing this spell somewhere safe, spend some time connecting with friends (old or new) and notice how your friendships deepen and expand.

## SPELL JAR RECIPE #5: A GLAMOR SPELL FOR INCREASING YOUR PERSONAL ATTRACTIVENESS

*A recipe for glamor (increasing your personal attractions)*

After cleansing your space, casting a spell circle if desired, and calling on any guides or intentions you feel drawn to, light a white, green, or pink spell candle with a match or lighter.

Then put the following ingredients in your jar:

- Pink Himalayan salt, rice, OR flax seeds
- Rose quartz, amethyst, OR ruby
- Pearl, moonstone, OR opal
- Apple OR strawberry (dried)
- Avocado (skin or seed)
- Geranium, rose, jasmine, OR ylang-ylang oil

- Cinnamon OR catnip
- A drop of milk
- Honey, sugar, OR maple syrup
- White, green, or pink ribbon and a white, green, or pink candle for sealing

Seal the bottle with a stopper if desired, then cover the seal with white, green, or pink wax and a white, green, or pink ribbon. Hold the bottle in your hands for a few moments, feeling the energy. If you choose, recite (out loud or in your mind) something like this:

*I call on my personal beauty with this jar*
*I embrace my inner glamor*
*And welcome the sure knowing*
*Of my own power*
*So it is*
*And so mote it be*

Keep the jar under your bed or near where you keep your clothes or makeup. You may wish to experiment with new styles or products if you have the time and money—so much of glamor is *believing* you are already beautiful! Any time you wear something that makes you feel fabulous, you are practicing magic.

## SPELL JAR RECIPE #6: A SPELL FOR BREAKUP RECOVERY

*A recipe for recovering from a breakup (platonic or romantic)*

After cleansing your space, casting a spell circle if desired, and calling on any guides or intentions you feel drawn to, light a green spell candle with a match or lighter.

Then put the following ingredients in your jar:

- Sand OR dirt
- Black tourmaline, hematite, OR onyx
- Amaranth, barley, OR rice
- Ivy, chicory, OR coriander
- Rose quartz, amethyst, OR selenite
- Malachite, emerald, OR bloodstone
- Beryl, pearl, OR moonstone
- Cyprus, fennel, OR eucalyptus oil
- Frankincense, myrrh, OR cedarwood oil
- Green ribbon and green candle for sealing

Seal the bottle with a stopper if desired, then cover the seal with yellow wax and yellow ribbon. Hold the bottle in your hands for a few moments, feeling the energy. If you choose, recite (out loud or in your mind) something like this:

*I am loved, loving, and lovable*
*Everything is as it should be*

After placing this spell somewhere safe, spend some time journaling about your feelings.

# CHAPTER 5
# SPELLS FOR PROSPERITY AND WEALTH

## SPELL JAR RECIPE #7: BREAKING FREE OF FINANCIAL BURDENS

*A recipe for releasing old money habits and patterns so new money systems can take their place*

After cleansing your space, casting a spell circle if desired, and calling on any guides or intentions you feel drawn to, light a green or gold spell candle with a match or lighter.

Then put the following ingredients in your jar:

- Salt (any color—black or gray preferred)
- Rice, beans, OR dried fruit
- Black tourmaline, hematite, OR onyx
- Pyrite, tiger's eye, OR citrine
- Malachite, emerald, OR bloodstone
- Bergamot OR patchouli oil
- Frankincense, myrrh, OR cedarwood oil
- Bay leaf, cinnamon, OR clove
- Ginger, cayenne, OR red pepper

- Coins, money, OR a check with a large sum written on it (made out to yourself)
- Green or gold ribbon and green or gold candle for sealing

Seal the bottle with a stopper if desired, then cover the seal with yellow wax and yellow ribbon. Hold the bottle in your hands for a few moments, feeling the energy. If you choose, recite (out loud or in your mind) something like this:

*I release everything keeping me in poverty and lack*
*I step into the financial freedom that is my birthright*
*Past, present, and future*
*So it is and so it shall be*

Place the jar in your purse, near where you keep your wallet, or on your desk where you sit to balance your checkbook or pay your bills. You may also wish to create a money manifesting altar where you keep this jar and some other totems designed to attract money. A money crystal grid is a great idea.

I also suggest doing this exercise, either before or after creating the spell jar:

- Take a scrap piece of paper and write down a list of any negative financial patterns you can think of (e.g., "not enough income," "compulsive spending," "fear of debt," etc.).
- Pay particular attention to any inherited or ancestral patterns tied to money (e.g., "divorce," "servitude," "Great Depression," "financial ruin," etc.) and write those down, too.
- Then setting an intention to remove these patterns completely, shred or burn the paper

and discard the pieces. Make sure it's totally destroyed. You are using your intention to release any energetic baggage keeping these things part of your life.
- Lastly, sit back and watch your money patterns shift! If you notice any weird money changes happening over the next few days, be patient and keep a positive mindset. Sometimes it takes a little bit of universal re-arranging as these things take effect.

I recommend accompanying this exercise with meditation, grounding, energy work, and other resources to increase your abundance. And don't forget to make a plan for financial prosperity—inspired action is the key!

## SPELL JAR RECIPE #8: MOTIVATION FOR IMPROVING YOUR LIFE CIRCUMSTANCES

*Sometimes it's hard to stay motivated when trying to level up. This recipe will help you stay focused and keep the faith.*

After cleansing your space, casting a spell circle if desired, and calling on any guides or intentions you feel drawn to, light a yellow or orange spell candle with a match or lighter.

Then put the following ingredients in your jar:

- Rocks, pebbles, OR gravel
- Onyx, hematite, OR black tourmaline
- Selenite, clear quartz, OR calcite
- Malachite, emerald, OR bloodstone
- Pyrite, tiger's eye, OR citrine
- Orange, lemon, OR lime peel

- Cabbage, cashew, OR carrot
- Peppermint OR fennel oil
- Clove, cardamom, OR allspice
- Ginger, cayenne, OR red pepper
- Moss, plant stem, OR snake skin (for transformation and growth)
- A list of motivational affirmations
- Yellow or orange ribbon and yellow or orange candle for sealing

Seal the bottle with a stopper if desired, then cover the seal with yellow wax and yellow ribbon. Hold the bottle in your hands for a few moments, feeling the energy. If you choose, recite (out loud or in your mind) something like this:

*I can do anything I set my mind to*
*As I envision it, so it shall be*
*And so it is*

Keep the jar in a safe place where it will remind you to stay strong and keep going.

## SPELL JAR RECIPE #9: FINDING A NEW JOB

*A recipe for finding new job opportunities, filling out applications, and doing well at job interviews*

After cleansing your space, casting a spell circle if desired, and calling on any guides or intentions you feel drawn to, light a blue spell candle with a match or lighter.

Then put the following ingredients in your jar:

- Rocks OR sand
- Onyx, hematite, OR black tourmaline
- Pyrite, tiger's eye, OR citrine

- Aquamarine, sodalite, OR jasper
- Jade, lapis lazuli, OR howlite
- Cyprus, fennel, OR eucalyptus oil
- Jasmine, ylang-ylang, OR rose oil
- Lemon, orange, OR lime oil
- Ginger, cayenne, OR red pepper
- Acorn, buckeye, OR bamboo
- Aloe, chestnut, OR hazel
- A description of your ideal job, written on an old paycheck or other paper representing money and success
- Sugar, honey, OR maple syrup
- Blue ribbon and blue candle for sealing

Seal the bottle with a stopper if desired, then cover the seal with blue wax and blue ribbon. Hold the bottle in your hands for a few moments, feeling the energy. If you choose, recite (out loud or in your mind) something like this:

*I love my new job*
*Finding a job is easy and fun*
*I'm learning to love what I do*
*What I do is learning to love me*
*Thank you, thank you, thank you*

Keep the jar in a safe place, perhaps where you fill out job applications or search for new opportunities. If practical, take the jar with you in your bag, pocket, or car as you interview. It might also help to do some journaling about your ideal job—if you could do *anything* in the world, what would you do? Describe it in detail. You can also make a vision board for the kind of job you would like and look at it daily while you search for a new job.

## SPELL JAR RECIPE #10: ATTRACT MONEY

*A recipe for allowing more money to flow into your life*

After cleansing your space, casting a spell circle if desired, and calling on any guides or intentions you feel drawn to, light a green or gold spell candle with a match or lighter.

Then put the following ingredients in your jar:

- Rocks OR sand
- Rice, beans, OR dried fruit
- Amaranth, barley, OR rice
- Cyprus, fennel, OR eucalyptus oil
- Pyrite, tiger's eye, OR citrine
- Malachite, emerald, OR bloodstone
- Bergamot OR patchouli oil
- Bay leaf, cinnamon, OR clove
- Ginger, cayenne, OR red pepper
- Coins, money, OR a check with a large sum written on it (made out to yourself)
- A feather (optional)
- A few drops of salt water
- Sugar, honey, OR maple syrup
- Green or gold ribbon and green or gold candle for sealing

Seal the bottle with a stopper if desired, then cover the seal with yellow wax and yellow ribbon. Hold the bottle in your hands for a few moments, feeling the energy. If you choose, recite (out loud or in your mind) something like this:

*Money flows to me every single day*
*I spend and receive freely, effortlessly, and with ease*

*Where my attention goes, my abundance flows*
*And so it is*

Place the jar in your purse, near where you keep your wallet, or on your desk where you sit to balance your checkbook or pay your bills. Then spend time just noticing all the money you receive—even if it's just seeing a penny on the street and picking it up. It might be helpful to start a gratitude journal to keep track of every time you receive anything of abundance. You can also say "thank you" to your money every time you spend or receive it (this is known as the "arigato method," and you can research it online). Pairing this spell with some inner work about your money worries and fears (as well as any ancestral patterns of lack) will be really helpful. Stand back and watch the money flow in!

## SPELL JAR RECIPE #11: PRODUCTIVITY

*A recipe for getting more done and maximizing your efforts*

After cleansing your space, casting a spell circle if desired, and calling on any guides or intentions you feel drawn to, light a green or gold spell candle with a match or lighter.

Then put the following ingredients in your jar:

- Rice, amaranth, OR beans
- Pyrite, tiger's eye, OR citrine
- Lemon, orange, OR lime peel
- Bergamot OR patchouli oil
- Clove, cinnamon, OR allspice
- Dandelion OR dandelion root
- Banana peel OR dried banana
- Orange ribbon and orange candle for sealing

Seal the bottle with a stopper if desired, then cover the seal with yellow wax and yellow ribbon. Hold the bottle in your hands for a few moments, feeling the energy. If you choose, recite (out loud or in your mind) something like this:

*Everything I set my mind to flows with ease*
*I call my power back to me now*
*And so it is*

Place the jar near where you work and look at it often to remember that you can do this!

## CHAPTER 6
# PROTECTION SPELLS

### SPELL JAR RECIPE #12: A GENERAL PROTECTION SPELL

*A basic recipe for general protection. Be sure to indicate what kind of protection you are looking for—mental, emotional, physical, or spiritual. Perhaps all of the above!*

After cleansing your space, casting a spell circle if desired, and calling on any guides or intentions you feel drawn to, light a black spell candle with a match or lighter.

Then put the following ingredients in your jar (remember, feel free to substitute any of these or leave out any that you can't find or if the bottle is too small):

- Small rocks OR gravel
- Garlic powder, garlic salt, dried garlic, OR garlic cloves
- Small nails, pins, thorns, thistles, OR cactus needles
- Bark OR part of a pinecone

- Frankincense, cedarwood, clary sage, OR tea tree essential oil (3-5 drops)
- Black tourmaline, hematite, onyx, OR lava stone

Seal the bottle with a stopper if desired, then cover the seal with black wax. Hold the bottle in your hands for a few moments, feeling the energy of it. If you choose, recite (out loud or in your mind) something like this:

*I am protected, I am safe, I am secure*
*So it is and so it shall be*

Keep this jar in a safe place in your home or near where you live. You can also choose to bury this jar in your yard or garden.

## SPELL JAR RECIPE #13: PHYSICAL SAFETY

*A recipe for physical safety, perhaps while at work or traveling.*

After cleansing your space, casting a spell circle if desired, and calling on any guides or intentions you feel drawn to, light a black spell candle with a match or lighter.

Then put the following ingredients in your jar (remember, feel free to substitute):

- Small black rocks, gravel, OR sand
- Black tourmaline, hematite, onyx, OR lava stone
- Selenite, howlite, OR clear quartz
- Tiger's eye, citrine, OR pyrite
- Needles, pins, tacks, thorns, OR cactus needles
- Nettle, thistle, OR parsley
- Cumin, garlic, red pepper, cinnamon, OR black pepper
- A small piece of paper or cloth with your special intention written on it (e.g., *"My dog is safe while*

*I am on vacation"* or *"My family is safe on their trip"*)

Seal the bottle with a stopper if desired, then cover the seal with black wax from the candle. Hold the bottle in your hands for a few moments, feeling the energy of it. Focus entirely on your special intention of protection for the person, place, animal, thing, idea, or whatever you are keeping safe. Keep your focus solely on this thing and how safe it is until you feel you have done enough (perhaps five minutes or so). Obviously, this spell will not work if you do something deliberately dangerous, so use it as an added boost for normal activities or to protect a loved one in need.

## SPELL JAR RECIPE #14: ENERGETIC PROTECTION SPELL

*A basic recipe for protection from other people's energy. Can be adapted for another friend or family member, or simply use it for yourself.*

After cleansing your space, casting a spell circle if desired, and calling on any guides or intentions you feel drawn to, light a purple spell candle with a match or lighter.

Then put the following ingredients in your jar (remember, feel free to substitute):

- Sand, dirt, fine gravel, OR black salt
- Small nails, pins, thorns, thistles, OR cactus needles
- Lavender, rose, sandalwood, OR cypress essential oil (3-5 drops)
- Rose quartz, amethyst, lepidolite, OR selenite

- Leaf from a rose, wild raspberry, blackberry, OR other similar plant
- A bay leaf OR small scrap of paper OR cloth, with the words *"I am an empowered empath"* written on it in black ink

Seal the bottle with a stopper if desired, then cover the seal with black wax. Hold the bottle in your hands for a few moments, feeling the energy of it. You may wish to repeat something like this, out loud or in your mind:

*I am me and you are you*
*I release all that is not me*
*I call back my power*

Keep this jar in a safe place until you feel its intention is fulfilled or that it's no longer working. At that point, you can choose whether to make a new spell jar or not.

## SPELL JAR RECIPE #15: PROTECTING YOUR HOME FOR SAFETY AND SECURITY

*A recipe for protecting your home from invaders and mishaps.*

After cleansing your space, casting a spell circle if desired, and calling on any guides or intentions you feel drawn to, light a black spell candle with a match or lighter.

Then put the following ingredients in your jar (remember, feel free to substitute):

- Sand, dirt, fine gravel, OR black salt
- Small nails, pins, thorns, thistles, OR cactus needles
- Sage, lavender, OR palo santo
- Bay, birch, OR cedar
- Cumin, clove, OR cinnamon

- Cedarwood, frankincense, OR myrrh oil
- A small piece of your home (perhaps a splinter of wood, a fallen nail, a small piece of rubble, or similar)
- Black spell candle and black ribbon

Seal the bottle with a stopper if desired, then cover the seal with black wax and a black ribbon. Hold the bottle in your hands for a few moments, feeling the energy of it. If you feel inclined, you might say something like this (out loud or in your mind):

*My home is safe and secure*
*All is well*
*I seal this jar and it is so*

Keep this jar in a safe place until you feel its intention is fulfilled or that it's no longer working. You may also wish to bury the jar at the perimeter of your land or keep it near an entrance if you feel so inclined, perhaps hiding the jar on the porch, near your mailbox, or even in the garage.

# CHAPTER 7
# SUCCESS SPELLS

## SPELL JAR RECIPE #16: A SPELL FOR CLEAR COMMUNICATION

*A recipe for improving your communication with others*

After cleansing your space, casting a spell circle if desired, and calling on any guides or intentions you feel drawn to, light a white or blue spell candle with a match or lighter.

Then put the following ingredients in your jar:

- Sea salt, pink Himalayan salt, OR Epsom salt
- Sodalite, aquamarine, OR lapis lazuli
- Jade, malachite, OR bloodstone
- Garnet, beryl, OR amethyst
- Allspice, cinnamon, OR nutmeg
- Clove, caraway, OR oregano
- Mint, thyme, OR dill
- Peppermint, eucalyptus, OR tea tree oil
- Your specific intention, written on a bay leaf

- White or blue ribbon and white or blue candle for sealing

Seal the bottle with a stopper if desired, then cover the seal with white or blue wax and a white or blue ribbon. Hold the bottle in your hands for a few moments, feeling the energy. If you choose, recite (out loud or in your mind) something like this:

*I speak my truth clearly*
*I am heard and understood*
*I listen with love and express my needs equally with others*
*I communicate clearly—past, present, and future*

Keep the jar somewhere safe and let it work its magic. You can also try journaling about your thoughts and feelings to get them out on paper before communicating them to someone else.

## SPELL JAR RECIPE #17: A SPELL FOR NAILING YOUR PRESENTATION

*A recipe for success when giving a public speech*

After cleansing your space, casting a spell circle if desired, and calling on any guides or intentions you feel drawn to, light a blue spell candle with a match or lighter.

Then put the following ingredients in your jar:

- Coffee grounds, flax, OR salt
- Beryl, carnelian, OR hematite
- Sodalite, aquamarine, OR lapis lazuli
- Allspice, cinnamon, OR nutmeg
- Clove, caraway, OR oregano
- Mint, thyme, OR dill
- A feather (optional)

- Your speech or speech topic written on paper (optional)
- Blue ribbon and blue candle for sealing

Seal the bottle with a stopper if desired, then cover the seal with blue wax and a blue ribbon. Hold the bottle in your hands for a few moments, feeling the energy. If you choose, recite (out loud or in your mind) something like this:

*My speech went smoothly, my true voice is heard*
*All is well*

You will want to spend some time visualizing your speech going flawlessly—and practicing, of course!—along with making the spell jar. Drawing a picture or writing down what it will look like for the whole thing to go splendidly is a great idea, too.

## SPELL JAR RECIPE #18: A SPELL FOR INCREASING COURAGE

*A recipe for courage to do what you know you need to do*

After cleansing your space, casting a spell circle if desired, and calling on any guides or intentions you feel drawn to, light a yellow or orange spell candle with a match or lighter.

Then put the following ingredients in your jar:

- Dirt OR salt (black or gray preferred)
- Hematite, black tourmaline, OR lavastone
- Tiger's eye, citrine, OR agate
- Rosemary, fennel, OR yarrow
- Cayenne, mustard, OR cumin
- Ginger, turmeric, OR allspice

- Lemon, orange, OR lime oil
- Cedarwood, cypress, OR sandalwood oil
- Your intention written on a bay leaf OR slip of paper
- Yellow or orange ribbon and an orange or yellow candle for sealing

Seal the bottle with a stopper if desired, then cover the seal with yellow or orange wax and a yellow or orange ribbon. Hold the bottle in your hands for a few moments, feeling the energy. If you choose, recite (out loud or in your mind) something like this:

*I am strength, I am power*
*What I need to do is already done*
*I release fear and I am free*
*Past, present, and future*

Make a plan for what you need to do...and then do it. You've got this.

## SPELL JAR RECIPE #19: A SPELL FOR GREATER SELF-CONFIDENCE

*A recipe for confidence*

After cleansing your space, casting a spell circle if desired, and calling on any guides or intentions you feel drawn to, light a yellow or orange spell candle with a match or lighter.

Then put the following ingredients in your jar:

- Dirt, coffee grounds, OR salt
- Tiger's eye, citrine, OR pyrite
- Beryl, amber, OR garnet
- Basil, fennel, OR tarragon

- Cayenne, mustard, OR cumin
- Ginger, turmeric, OR allspice
- Lemon, orange, OR lime oil
- Yellow or orange ribbon and an orange or yellow candle for sealing

Seal the bottle with a stopper if desired, then cover the seal with yellow or orange wax and a yellow or orange ribbon. Hold the bottle in your hands for a few moments, feeling the energy. If you choose, recite (out loud or in your mind) something like this:

*I am confident*
*Everything works out for me*
*I speak the future into the past*
*And so it is*

Go after what you want with confidence! It is already yours.

## SPELL JAR RECIPE #20: A SPELL FOR CLEAR THINKING AND MENTAL FOCUS

*A recipe for clarity of mind, perhaps for making a decision or dealing with brain fog*

After cleansing your space, casting a spell circle if desired, and calling on any guides or intentions you feel drawn to, light a white or purple spell candle with a match or lighter.

Then put the following ingredients in your jar:

- Sea salt, pink Himalayan salt, OR Epsom salt
- Amethyst, lepidolite, OR fluorite
- Selenite, clear quartz, OR howlite
- Sage, rosemary, OR thyme

- Cayenne, mustard, OR cumin
- Ginger, cypress, OR patchouli oil
- Eucalyptus, tea tree, OR peppermint oil
- Frankincense, myrrh, OR cedarwood oil
- White or purple ribbon and a white or purple candle for sealing

Seal the bottle with a stopper if desired, then cover the seal with white or purple wax and a white or purple ribbon. Hold the bottle in your hands for a few moments, feeling the energy. If you choose, recite (out loud or in your mind) something like this:

*My mind is clear, and I am free*
*So it is, and so it shall be*

Keep the jar under your bed or near your pillow while you sleep or near your desk while you work. You can also practice mindfulness and deep breathing techniques to increase mental clarity.

## SPELL JAR RECIPE #21: A SPELL FOR MORE HOPE

*A recipe for increasing hope*

After cleansing your space, casting a spell circle if desired, and calling on any guides or intentions you feel drawn to, light a white or pink spell candle with a match or lighter.

Then put the following ingredients in your jar:

- Dirt, gravel, OR stones
- Selenite, clear quartz, OR howlite
- Opal, pearl, OR moonstone
- Sunflower, dandelion, OR passionflower
- Nutmeg, cinnamon, OR clove

- Lemon, orange, OR lime oil
- Frankincense, myrrh, OR cedarwood oil
- White or pink ribbon and a white or pink candle for sealing

Seal the bottle with a stopper if desired, then cover the seal with white or pink wax and a white or pink ribbon. Hold the bottle in your hands for a few moments, feeling the energy. If you choose, recite (out loud or in your mind) something like this:

*I am filled with hope*
*All is bright and at peace*

Keep the jar somewhere you need extra hope, such as by your bed, at work, or in your pocket or purse. You can also burn palo santo, sage, or lemongrass incense while you create the jar.

## SPELL JAR RECIPE #22: A SPELL FOR INCREASING YOUR LUCK

*A recipe to make you luckier!*

After cleansing your space, casting a spell circle if desired, and calling on any guides or intentions you feel drawn to, light a yellow or green spell candle with a match or lighter.

Then put the following ingredients in your jar:

- Rice, quinoa, sunflower seeds, OR amaranth
- Jade, jasper, OR carnelian
- Tiger's eye, citrine, OR pyrite
- Peridot, beryl, OR garnet
- Strawberry, apricot, OR banana (leaf or dried fruit)

- Nutmeg, cinnamon, OR clove
- Lemon, orange, OR lime oil
- Four leaf clover, favorite piece of jewelry, a coin, or other luck token (optional)
- A slip of paper with your intention written on it
- Yellow or green ribbon and a yellow or green candle for sealing

Seal the bottle with a stopper if desired, then cover the seal with yellow or green wax and a yellow or green ribbon. Hold the bottle in your hands for a few moments, feeling the energy. If you choose, recite (out loud or in your mind) something like this:

*Everything works out for me*
*The universe conspires in my favor*
*I was born under a lucky star*
*Past, present, and future*
*I seal this jar and it is so*

Keep the jar somewhere you need extra luck, such as by your bed, at work, or in your pocket or purse. You can also spend time thinking about all the lucky things that have happened to you, or even researching really lucky people and thinking what it will be like when you are lucky, too!

# CHAPTER 8
# TRANQUILITY SPELLS

### SPELL JAR RECIPE #23: AN ANTI-ANXIETY SPELL

*A recipe to soothe anxiety of all kinds*

After cleansing your space, casting a spell circle if desired, and calling on any guides or intentions you feel drawn to, light a white or silver spell candle with a match or lighter.

Then put the following ingredients in your jar:

- Sea salt, pink Himalayan salt, OR Epsom salt
- Hematite, onyx, OR black tourmaline
- Lavastone, obsidian, OR smoky quartz
- Amethyst, rose quartz, OR lepidolite
- Selenite, clear quartz, OR howlite
- Chamomile, St. John's wort, OR valerian
- Lavender, melissa, OR geranium oil
- Bergamot, patchouli, OR petitgrain oil
- Frankincense, myrrh, OR cedarwood oil
- White or silver ribbon and a white or silver candle for sealing

Seal the bottle with a stopper if desired, then cover the seal with white or silver wax and a white or green ribbon. Hold the bottle in your hands for a few moments, feeling the energy. If you choose, recite (out loud or in your mind) something like this:

*I release my fears and I am free*
*No matter what, I am safe and secure*
*All I need and want is with me now*
*And so it is, past, present, and future*

Keep the jar somewhere special to let it do its thing in the background, such as on a shelf or in your closet or under your bed. You can also try meditation, journaling, talking to a trusted friend or professional, and using relaxation techniques such as herbal teas and essential oils to boost the effects.

## SPELL JAR RECIPE #24: A SPELL FOR ACCEPTANCE

*A recipe to help you accept that which you cannot change and more forward in peace*

After cleansing your space, casting a spell circle if desired, and calling on any guides or intentions you feel drawn to, light a pink or silver spell candle with a match or lighter.

Then put the following ingredients in your jar:

- Dirt, pebbles, OR gravel
- Hematite, onyx, OR black tourmaline
- Selenite, clear quartz, OR howlite
- Pearl, opal, OR moonstone
- Lepidolite, amethyst, OR garnet
- Rosemary, thyme, OR sage
- Mustard, ginger, OR cumin

- Cinnamon, nutmeg, OR allspice
- Frankincense, myrrh, OR cedarwood oil
- A drop of salt water
- Intention, written on a slip of paper
- Pink or silver ribbon and a pink or silver candle for sealing

Seal the bottle with a stopper if desired, then cover the seal with pink or silver wax and a pink or silver ribbon. Hold the bottle in your hands for a few moments, feeling the energy. If you choose, recite (out loud or in your mind) something like this:

*Everything happens for a reason*
*I change what I cannot accept*
*I accept what I cannot change*
*It all works together for my highest and best good*
*Past, present, and future*

Keep the jar somewhere special to let it do its thing in the background, such as on a shelf or in your closet or under your bed. You can also bury it as a sign that you are burying the thing you are letting go of. Journaling about what you wish to accept can also be very helpful.

## SPELL JAR RECIPE #25: AN ANTI-DEPRESSION SPELL

*A recipe to relieve some of the symptoms of depression*

After cleansing your space, casting a spell circle if desired, and calling on any guides or intentions you feel drawn to, light a gold or silver spell candle with a match or lighter.

Then put the following ingredients in your jar:

- Dirt, pebbles, OR gravel

- Hematite, onyx, OR black tourmaline
- Lavastone, obsidian, OR smoky quartz
- Selenite, clear quartz, OR howlite
- Pearl, opal, OR moonstone
- Lepidolite, amethyst, OR fluorite
- Rosemary, thyme, OR sage
- Lavender, melissa, OR geranium oil
- Lemon, orange, OR lime oil
- Frankincense, myrrh, OR cedarwood oil
- Intention written on a bay leaf
- Gold or silver ribbon and a gold or silver candle for sealing

Seal the bottle with a stopper if desired, then cover the seal with gold or silver wax and a gold or silver ribbon. Hold the bottle in your hands for a few moments, feeling the energy. If you choose, recite (out loud or in your mind) something like this:

*I love myself, just as I am*
*I offer myself concern and compassion every day*
*I take it slowly, one day at a time*
*Gently, lovingly, I take back my power*
*I seal this jar and it is so*

Keep the jar somewhere special to let it do its thing in the background, such as on a shelf or in your closet or under your bed. You should always get the professional help you need whenever dealing with symptoms of depression.

## SPELL JAR RECIPE #26: A SPELL FOR FORGIVENESS

*A recipe for forgiving those who have hurt you*

After cleansing your space, casting a spell circle if desired, and calling on any guides or intentions you feel drawn to, light a white or green spell candle with a match or lighter.

Then put the following ingredients in your jar:

- Sea salt, pink Himalayan salt, OR Epsom salt
- Hematite, onyx, OR black tourmaline
- Emerald, malachite, OR bloodstone
- Opal, pearl, OR moonstone
- Aquamarine, azurite, OR sodalite
- Amethyst, rose quartz, OR garnet
- Selenite, clear quartz, OR howlite
- Rose, jasmine, OR ylang-ylang oil
- Frankincense, myrrh, OR cedarwood oil
- Three drops of salt water
- White or green ribbon and a white or green candle for sealing

Seal the bottle with a stopper if desired, then cover the seal with white or green wax and a white or green ribbon. Hold the bottle in your hands for a few moments, feeling the energy. If you choose, recite (out loud or in your mind) something like this:

*I am me and you are you*
*What you did to me flows away like water*
*I am free to be me and you are free to be you*
*And so it is*

Keep the jar somewhere special to let it do its thing in the background, such as on a shelf or in your closet. Please always remember that you never need to forgive someone until you are ready; this spell merely helps you set your focus on releasing what you can so you can move on when the time is right. If letting go sooner rather than later is healthiest for you, this jar can help. Journaling your feelings, writing them an honest letter (which you can choose to burn instead of send), and talking to a trusted friend can also help the forgiveness process. Also remember that forgiving does not mean putting up with abuse. If someone continues to hurt you, you can remove yourself from the situation, set healthy boundaries, and still forgive when the time is right.

## SPELL JAR RECIPE #27: A SPELL FOR INNER PEACE AND SERENITY

*A recipe for finding your zen*

After cleansing your space, casting a spell circle if desired, and calling on any guides or intentions you feel drawn to, light a white or purple spell candle with a match or lighter.

Then put the following ingredients in your jar:

- Sea salt, pink Himalayan salt, OR Epsom salt
- Hematite, onyx, OR black tourmaline
- Opal, pearl, OR moonstone
- Amethyst, rose quartz, OR garnet
- Selenite, clear quartz, OR howlite
- Coriander, sage, OR oregano
- Rose, jasmine, OR ylang-ylang oil
- Frankincense, myrrh, OR cedarwood oil
- Zen symbols (such as om, enso, a lotus, yin and yang, etc.) written on a slip of paper
- White or purple ribbon and a white or purple candle for sealing

Seal the bottle with a stopper if desired, then cover the seal with white or green wax and a white or purple ribbon.

Hold the bottle in your hands for a few moments, feeling the energy. If you choose, recite (out loud or in your mind) something like this:

*I am One with All That Is*
*I am at peace*
*And so it is*

Keep the jar somewhere you need extra peace and serenity, such as near your bed, by your desk, or in your pocket or purse. Meditation, walking in nature, getting a massage or Reiki session, journaling, eating healthy, exercising, being in or near water, taking a salt bath, and other self-care methods can also help with inner serenity and peace.

## CHAPTER 9
# HEALTH SPELLS

SPELL JAR RECIPE #28: A SPELL FOR EMOTIONAL HEALING

*A recipe for healing the heart, as well as the body and the mind*

After cleansing your space, casting a spell circle if desired, and calling on any guides or intentions you feel drawn to, light a green or white spell candle with a match or lighter.

Then put the following ingredients in your jar:

- Sea salt, pink Himalayan salt, OR Epsom salts
- Malachite, emerald, OR bloodstone
- Rose quartz, moonstone, OR peridot
- Fennel, rosemary, OR thyme
- Red pepper, black pepper, OR cayenne pepper
- Cypress, spruce, OR juniper berry oil
- Lime, lemongrass, OR eucalyptus oil
- Rose, geranium, OR ylang-ylang oil
- Green or white ribbon and a green or white candle for sealing

Seal the bottle with a stopper if desired, then cover the seal with green or white wax and a green or white ribbon. Hold the bottle in your hands for a few moments, feeling the energy. If you choose, recite (out loud or in your mind) something like this:

*I honor my emotions and I am free*
*I seal this jar and so it is*

Keep the jar anywhere it can work its magic in the background, perhaps near your crystals or on your bedside table.

## SPELL JAR RECIPE #29: A SPELL FOR FERTILITY

*A recipe for increasing your chances of conceiving*

After cleansing your space, casting a spell circle if desired, and calling on any guides or intentions you feel drawn to, light a green, orange, red, or white spell candle with a match or lighter.

Then put the following ingredients in your jar:

- Sea salt, pink Himalayan salt, OR Epsom salts
- Carnelian, jasper, OR citrine
- Moonstone, pearl, OR opal
- Apple, banana, OR strawberry (dried)
- Chickweed, plantain, OR clover
- Cabbage OR carrot
- Hawthorne, hazel, OR mistletoe
- Parsley, sage, OR rosemary
- Cinnamon, mint, OR coriander
- Bergamot, patchouli, OR petitgrain oil
- Sandalwood, clary sage, OR lemongrass oil
- Ylang-ylang, geranium, OR jasmine oil

- A small baby item, such as a shoe, hair bow, or yarn from a baby blanket
- Green, orange, red, or white ribbon and a green, orange, red or white candle for sealing

Seal the bottle with a stopper if desired, then cover the seal with green, orange, red, or white wax and a green, orange, red, or white ribbon. Hold the bottle in your hands for a few moments, feeling the energy. If you choose, recite (out loud or in your mind) something like this:

*I release my fears and I am free*
*I heal my womb and it heals me*
*I now conceive when the time is right*
*I call in my child now*
*Thank you for choosing me to be your mother*

Keep the jar anywhere it can work its magic in the background, perhaps near your crystals or on your altar. I'm sure you're already doing this, but whatever herbal, medical, or other steps you are taking to conceive, don't give up! Remember you are already a mother—to your friends, to your home, to the Earth. Your spiritual child is already with you and will be with you in the flesh when the time is right.

## SPELL JAR RECIPE #30: A SPELL FOR GOOD SLEEP

*A recipe for improving sleep and reducing insomnia*

After cleansing your space, casting a spell circle if desired, and calling on any guides or intentions you feel drawn to, light a white or purple spell candle with a match or lighter.

Then put the following ingredients in your jar:

- Dirt, gravel, OR stones
- Black tourmaline, hematite, OR onyx
- Selenite, clear quartz, OR howlite
- Lepidolite, amethyst, OR fluorite
- Chamomile, valerian, OR St. John's wort
- Lavender, vetiver, OR melissa oil
- Cypress, juniper berry, OR spruce oil
- Frankincense, myrrh, OR cedarwood oil
- White or purple ribbon and a white or purple candle for sealing

Seal the bottle with a stopper if desired, then cover the seal with white or purple wax and a white or purple ribbon. Hold the bottle in your hands for a few moments, feeling the energy. If you choose, recite (out loud or in your mind) something like this:

*I release the fear of insomnia*
*I choose many forms of rest*
*As I relax, my body sleeps naturally*
*I am at rest*

Keep the jar under your bed beneath where your pillow is or in your bedside cabinet or table. You can also use meditation, herbal teas, essential oils, yoga, healing music, and other methods to improve your sleep. You can also try journaling your feelings before bedtime to calm any racing thoughts before trying to go to sleep.

## SPELL JAR RECIPE #31: A SPELL FOR GOOD DREAMS

*A recipe for reducing nightmares and increasing happy, gentle dreams*

After cleansing your space, casting a spell circle if desired, and calling on any guides or intentions you feel drawn to, light a white or silver spell candle with a match or lighter.

Then put the following ingredients in your jar:

- Dirt, gravel, OR pebbles
- Pins, nails, OR thorns
- Black tourmaline, hematite, OR onyx
- Selenite, clear quartz, OR howlite
- Lepidolite, amethyst, OR moonstone
- Chamomile, valerian, OR St. John's wort
- Lavender, vetiver, OR melissa oil
- Cypress, juniper berry, OR spruce oil
- Frankincense, myrrh, OR cedarwood oil
- Sugar, honey, OR maple syrup
- White or silver ribbon and a white or silver candle for sealing

Seal the bottle with a stopper if desired, then cover the seal with white or silver wax and a white or silver ribbon. Hold the bottle in your hands for a few moments, feeling the energy. If you choose, recite (out loud or in your mind) something like this:

*I release my fears and I am free*
*I welcome all good dreams*
*I release the past and walk into the future*
*I seal this jar and so it is*

Keep the jar under your bed beneath where your pillow is or in your bedside cabinet or table. You can also keep a journal by your bed to record your dreams and see if you can find any hidden meanings in them. A wise witch knows that her soul speaks to her at night, so sometimes acknowledging what your dreams are trying to tell you can really help. You can also pay attention to the moon phases and make note of any patterns, as well as see a professional dream interpreter for guidance.

## SPELL JAR RECIPE #32: CLEAR, FLAWLESS SKIN JAR SPELL

*A recipe for clear skin*

After cleansing your space, casting a spell circle if desired, and calling on any guides or intentions you feel drawn to, light a white or red spell candle with a match or lighter.

Then put the following ingredients in your jar:

- Sea salt, pink Himalayan salt, OR Epsom salt
- Rose quartz, amethyst, OR ruby
- Selenite, clear quartz, OR howlite
- Yarrow, elder, OR dandelion root
- Eucalyptus, tea tree, OR peppermint oil
- Geranium, rose, jasmine, OR ylang-ylang oil
- Frankincense, myrrh, OR cedarwood oil
- "I love my clear skin" written on a bay leaf
- White or red ribbon and a white or red candle for sealing

Seal the bottle with a stopper if desired, then cover the seal with white or red wax and a white or red ribbon. Hold the bottle in your hands for a few moments, feeling the energy. If you choose, recite (out loud or in your mind) something like this:

*My skin is clear as glass*
*I release all fear, anger, and doubt*
*I am beautiful just as I am*
*I seal this jar and it is so*

Keep the jar under your bed or near your pillow while you sleep or near where you do your nightly face routine. You can also practice visualizations and affirmations for clear skin.

## SPELL JAR RECIPE #33: A SPELL FOR BOOSTING YOUR ENERGY AND MOTIVATION

*A recipe for greater energy and motivation*

After cleansing your space, casting a spell circle if desired, and calling on any guides or intentions you feel drawn to, light a yellow or orange spell candle with a match or lighter.

Then put the following ingredients in your jar:

- Coffee, green tea, OR black tea
- Hematite, black tourmaline, OR lavastone
- Tiger's eye, pyrite, OR citrine
- Ginger, turmeric, OR cumin
- Cinnamon, nutmeg, OR clove
- Cayenne, red pepper, OR black pepper
- Peppermint, eucalyptus, OR tea tree oil
- Lemon, lime, OR orange oil
- Affirmations written on a slip of paper
- Yellow or orange ribbon and a yellow or orange candle for sealing

Seal the bottle with a stopper if desired, then cover the seal with yellow or orange wax and a yellow or orange ribbon. Hold the bottle in your hands for a few moments, feeling the energy. If you choose, recite (out loud or in your mind) something like this:

*I welcome motivation and energy*

*I can do anything I set my mind to*
*And so it is*

Keep the jar somewhere it can work its magic in the background, perhaps on your desk or in your kitchen. Sometimes a lack of energy or motivation comes from physical or mental health challenges, so doing what you need to do to feel better is an important step, as well!

## SPELL JAR RECIPE #34: A SPELL FOR PAIN RELIEF

*A recipe for relieving chronic or other types of physical pain*

After cleansing your space, casting a spell circle if desired, and calling on any guides or intentions you feel drawn to, light a green or white spell candle with a match or lighter.

Then put the following ingredients in your jar:

- Sea salt, pink Himalayan salt, OR Epsom salts
- Hematite, black tourmaline, OR lavastone
- Amber, citrine, OR carnelian
- Malachite, emerald, OR bloodstone
- Selenite, clear quartz, OR howlite
- Ginger, turmeric, OR cumin
- Cayenne, red pepper, OR black pepper
- Anise, fennel, OR coriander
- Cinnamon, nutmeg, OR clove
- Peppermint, eucalyptus, OR tea tree oil
- Lemon, lime, OR orange oil
- Intention written on a slip of paper
- A drop of salt water
- Green or white ribbon and a green or white candle for sealing

Seal the bottle with a stopper if desired, then cover the seal with green or white wax and a green or white ribbon. Hold the bottle in your hands for a few moments, feeling the energy. If you choose, recite (out loud or in your mind) something like this:

*I release my pain and I am free*
*I welcome healing and peace*
*And so it is*

Keep the jar somewhere it can work its magic in the background, perhaps near your bed while you sleep or near your desk while you work.

## SPELL JAR RECIPE #35: A GROUNDING SPELL

*A recipe for connecting to Mother Earth to increase grounding, connection, and healing. Can also increase abundance.*

After cleansing your space, casting a spell circle if desired, and calling on any guides or intentions you feel drawn to, light a green or brown spell candle with a match or lighter.

Then put the following ingredients in your jar:

- Dirt, gravel, OR stones
- Black tourmaline, hematite, OR onyx
- Lavastone, shungite, OR obsidian
- Acorn, chestnut, OR buckeye
- Potato, beet, OR carrot
- Dandelion root, ginger, OR coffee
- Bergamot, patchouli, OR petitgrain oil
- Cypress, spruce, OR cedarwood oil
- Clary sage, juniper berry, OR lavender oil
- Green or brown ribbon and a green or brown candle for sealing

Seal the bottle with a stopper if desired, then cover the seal with green or brown wax and a green or brown ribbon. Hold the bottle in your hands for a few moments, feeling the energy. If you choose, recite (out loud or in your mind) something like this:

*I am connected to Mother Earth*
*I am grounded*
*I am strong*
*Like the roots of a tree, I stand in my own power*
*Mother Earth watches over me*
*And so it is*

Keep the jar near where you do your yoga or meditation, or perhaps in your kitchen or living room where you relax and spend time with your family or "tribe." Spend as much time as you can outside with your bare feet on the earth, or even lying on the grass (or perhaps even on a special "earthing" sheet you can buy online). Grounding meditations and music can be very helpful for grounding as well!

## CHAPTER 10
# BANISHMENT SPELLS

SPELL JAR RECIPE #36: A GENERAL BANISHING SPELL

*A basic recipe for general banishment. Be sure to indicate what you are banishing and be very clear on who—or what—you want to cast out of your life.*

After cleansing your space, casting a spell circle if desired, and calling on any guides or intentions you feel drawn to, light a black spell candle with a match or lighter.

Then put the following ingredients in your jar (remember, feel free to substitute any of these or leave out any that you can't find or if the bottle is too small):

- Small rocks OR gravel
- Black tourmaline, shungite, OR onyx
- Obsidian, lavastone, OR hematite
- Garlic, chives, OR onion
- Nettle, parsley, OR thistle
- Black pepper
- Salt

- Small nails, pins, thorns, thistles, OR cactus needles
- Frankincense, cedarwood, clary sage, OR myrrh essential oil
- A slip of paper with the person or thing you want to banish written on it
- A black spell candle and black ribbon for sealing

Seal the bottle with a stopper if desired, then cover the seal with black wax. Hold the bottle in your hands for a few moments, feeling the energy of it. If you choose, recite (out loud or in your mind) something like this:

*I banish you from my life*
*I seal this jar and it is so*

Keep this jar in a safe place in your home or near where you live. You can also choose to bury this jar in your yard or garden.

## SPELL JAR RECIPE #37: A SPELL FOR BANISHING FATIGUE

*A recipe for banishing fatigue*

After cleansing your space, casting a spell circle if desired, and calling on any guides or intentions you feel drawn to, light a black spell candle with a match or lighter.

Then put the following ingredients in your jar (remember, feel free to substitute any of these or leave out any that you can't find or if the bottle is too small):

- Small rocks OR gravel
- Black tourmaline, shungite, OR onyx
- Obsidian, lavastone, OR hematite
- Garlic, chives, OR onion

- Cinnamon, cumin, OR nutmeg
- Dried eggshells, tree bark, OR dried bits of pinecone
- Lemon, orange, OR lime essential oil
- Frankincense, cedarwood, clary sage, OR myrrh essential oil
- A black spell candle and black ribbon for sealing

Seal the bottle with a stopper if desired, then cover the seal with black wax. Hold the bottle in your hands for a few moments, feeling the energy of it. If you choose, recite (out loud or in your mind) something like this:

*I banish fatigue from my life*
*I release the sources of fatigue*
*And call back my power from the four corners of the world*
*I seal this jar and it is so*

Keep this jar in a safe place in your home or near where you sleep. You can also choose to bury this jar in your yard or garden.

## SPELL JAR RECIPE #38: A SPELL FOR BANISHING CHILDHOOD TRAUMA

*A recipe for banishing the trauma patterns you received in childhood. Can be used for generational healing.*

After cleansing your space, casting a spell circle if desired, and calling on any guides or intentions you feel drawn to, light a black spell candle with a match or lighter.

Then put the following ingredients in your jar (remember, feel free to substitute any of these or leave out any that you can't find or if the bottle is too small):

- Sea salt, pink Himalayan salt, OR Epsom salt

- Black tourmaline, shungite, OR onyx
- Obsidian, lavastone, OR hematite
- Malachite, emerald, OR bloodstone
- Rose quartz, amethyst, OR lepidolite
- Selenite, clear quartz, OR howlite
- Garlic, chives, OR onion
- Black pepper, red pepper, OR cayenne
- Cinnamon, cumin, OR nutmeg
- Dried eggshells, tree bark, OR dried bits of pinecone
- Lavender, clary sage, OR lemon oil
- Frankincense, cedarwood, clary sage, OR myrrh essential oil
- A black spell candle and black ribbon for sealing

Seal the bottle with a stopper if desired, then cover the seal with black wax. Hold the bottle in your hands for a few moments, feeling the energy of it. If you choose, recite (out loud or in your mind) something like this:

*I banish my past, I banish my past, I banish my past*
*And I am free*
*I welcome a new life*
*I remove childhood trauma from my past, present, and future*
*And all is well*

Keep this jar in a safe place in your home or near where you live. You can also choose to bury this jar in your yard or garden, or if it's available to you, near your childhood home (only if no one will see you do this!).

## SPELL JAR RECIPE #39: A SPELL FOR BANISHING NERVOUSNESS

*A recipe for banishing nervousness (perhaps before a date, a presentation, a new day at work or school...or any other time you need to keep the nervousness away).*

After cleansing your space, casting a spell circle if desired, and calling on any guides or intentions you feel drawn to, light a black spell candle with a match or lighter.

Then put the following ingredients in your jar (remember, feel free to substitute any of these or leave out any that you can't find or if the bottle is too small):

- Dirt, gravel, OR coffee grounds
- Black tourmaline, shungite, OR onyx
- Obsidian, lavastone, OR hematite
- Selenite, clear quartz, OR howlite
- Tiger's eye, citrine, OR pyrite
- Sodalite, aquamarine, OR jade
- Garlic, chives, OR onion
- Black pepper, red pepper, OR cayenne
- Cinnamon, cumin, OR nutmeg
- Dried eggshells, tree bark, OR dried bits of pinecone
- Frankincense, cedarwood, clary sage, OR myrrh essential oil
- A black spell candle and black ribbon for sealing

Seal the bottle with a stopper if desired, then cover the seal with black wax. Hold the bottle in your hands for a few moments, feeling the energy of it. If you choose, recite (out loud or in your mind) something like this:

*I banish my fears and trepidations*

*I command nervousness to leave my life*
*I ask for peace and confidence*
*And so it is*

Keep this jar in a safe place in your home or in your purse or pocket.

## SPELL JAR RECIPE #40: A SPELL FOR BANISHING NIGHTMARES

*A recipe for banishing nightmares*

After cleansing your space, casting a spell circle if desired, and calling on any guides or intentions you feel drawn to, light a black spell candle with a match or lighter.

Then put the following ingredients in your jar (remember, feel free to substitute any of these or leave out any that you can't find or if the bottle is too small):

- Sea salt, pink Himalayan salt, OR Epsom salt
- Black tourmaline, shungite, OR onyx
- Obsidian, lavastone, OR hematite
- Rose quartz, amethyst, OR lepidolite
- Selenite, clear quartz, OR howlite
- Garlic, chives, OR onion
- Chamomile, valerian, OR St. John's wort
- Black pepper, red pepper, OR cayenne
- Cinnamon, cumin, OR nutmeg
- Dried eggshells, tree bark, OR dried bits of pinecone
- Lavender, clary sage, OR lemon oil
- Frankincense, cedarwood, clary sage, OR myrrh essential oil
- A black spell candle and black ribbon for sealing

Seal the bottle with a stopper if desired, then cover the seal with black wax. Hold the bottle in your hands for a few moments, feeling the energy of it. If you choose, recite (out loud or in your mind) something like this:

*I banish nightmares and I am free*
*I banish all fear and I am safe*
*I banish the darkness and I am made of loving light*
*And so it is, past, present, and future*

Keep this jar near where you sleep, perhaps under your bed beneath where your pillow is, between your bed and the wall, on your bedside table, or in your bedside cabinet.

## SPELL JAR RECIPE #41: A SPELL FOR BANISHING OVERTHINKING

*A recipe for banishing overthinking*

After cleansing your space, casting a spell circle if desired, and calling on any guides or intentions you feel drawn to, light a black spell candle with a match or lighter.

Then put the following ingredients in your jar (remember, feel free to substitute any of these or leave out any that you can't find or if the bottle is too small):

- Sea salt, pink Himalayan salt, OR Epsom salt
- Black tourmaline, shungite, OR onyx
- Obsidian, lavastone, OR hematite
- Clear quartz, amethyst, OR lepidolite
- Garlic, chives, OR onion
- Rosemary, fennel, OR coriander
- Dried eggshells, tree bark, OR dried bits of pinecone
- Lavender, clary sage, OR lemon oil

- Frankincense, cedarwood, clary sage, OR myrrh essential oil
- A black spell candle and black ribbon for sealing

Seal the bottle with a stopper if desired, then cover the seal with black wax. Hold the bottle in your hands for a few moments, feeling the energy of it. If you choose, recite (out loud or in your mind) something like this:

*I banish overthinking*
*I move into my body and out of my head*
*Everything happens just as it should*
*I banish overthinking and I am free*

Keep this jar near where you work, sleep, or relax in the evening, perhaps in your living room, your kitchen, by your bed, or by your desk at work.

## SPELL JAR RECIPE #42: A SPELL FOR BANISHING EVIL

*A recipe for banishing evil in your home, your workplace, your car, or anywhere else.*

After cleansing your space, casting a spell circle if desired, and calling on any guides or intentions you feel drawn to, light a black or purple spell candle with a match or lighter.

Then put the following ingredients in your jar (remember, feel free to substitute any of these or leave out any that you can't find or if the bottle is too small):

- Dirt, gravel, OR pebbles
- Sea salt, pink Himalayan salt, OR Epsom salt
- Black tourmaline, shungite, OR onyx
- Clear quartz, selenite, OR lepidolite

- Nettle, parsley, OR thistle
- Garlic, chives, OR onion
- Dried eggshells, tree bark, OR dried bits of pinecone
- Frankincense, cedarwood, clary sage, OR myrrh essential oil
- A black or purple spell candle and a black or purple ribbon for sealing

Seal the bottle with a stopper if desired, then cover the seal with black or purple wax. Hold the bottle in your hands for a few moments, feeling the energy of it. If you choose, recite (out loud or in your mind) something like this:

*I banish evil from my home and from my life*
*I now choose to walk in the light*
*I cleanse this place and it is made new*
*And so it is*

Keep this jar somewhere safe and secure, perhaps in the back of a closet, in the cellar or basement of your home, or buried in the corner of your property. If you live in an apartment, under the sink or behind a piece of furniture will also do.

## SPELL JAR RECIPE #43: A SPELL FOR BANISHING LIES

*A recipe for banishing the lies people tell you and the people who tell you lies*

After cleansing your space, casting a spell circle if desired, and calling on any guides or intentions you feel drawn to, light a black spell candle with a match or lighter.

Then put the following ingredients in your jar (remember, feel free to substitute any of these or leave out any that you can't find or if the bottle is too small):

- Sea salt, pink Himalayan salt, OR Epsom salt
- Hematite, shungite, OR obsidian
- Tiger's eye, agate, OR citrine
- Sodalite, aquamarine, OR garnet
- Garlic, chives, OR onion
- Dried eggshells, tree bark, OR dried bits of pinecone
- Peppermint, eucalyptus, OR tea tree oil
- Frankincense, cedarwood, clary sage, OR myrrh essential oil
- A black spell candle and black ribbon for sealing

Seal the bottle with a stopper if desired, then cover the seal with black wax. Hold the bottle in your hands for a few moments, feeling the energy of it. If you choose, recite (out loud or in your mind) something like this:

*I banish liars, lying, and lies*
*And so it is*

Keep this jar somewhere safe, perhaps near your altar or where you keep your crystals. Alternately, you can carry it with you to ward off liars and lying throughout your day.

## SPELL JAR RECIPE #44: A SPELL FOR BANISHING UNWANTED PEOPLE

*A recipe for banishing the people who no longer serve you. Be sure to be very clear on which people you wish to banish—they may disappear silently or dramatically, so be prepared!*

After cleansing your space, casting a spell circle if desired, and calling on any guides or intentions you feel drawn to, light a black spell candle with a match or lighter.

Then put the following ingredients in your jar

(remember, feel free to substitute any of these or leave out any that you can't find or if the bottle is too small):

- Dirt, gravel, OR coffee grounds
- Sea salt, pink Himalayan salt, OR Epsom salt
- Hematite, shungite, OR obsidian
- Garlic, chives, OR onion
- Dried eggshells, tree bark, OR dried bits of pinecone
- Frankincense, cedarwood, clary sage, OR myrrh essential oil
- Three drops of the vinegar of your choice (white vinegar, apple cider vinegar, rice vinegar, red wine vinegar, black vinegar…etc.)
- A slip of paper with the specific names of the people you want to banish, OR simply the kind of person you want to banish (e.g., "energy vampires," "cheats, "scammers," etc.)
- A black spell candle and black ribbon for sealing

Seal the bottle with a stopper if desired, then cover the seal with black wax. Hold the bottle in your hands for a few moments, feeling the energy of it. If you choose, recite (out loud or in your mind) something like this:

*I banish you from my life*
*You are no longer welcome*
*And I am free*

Keep this jar somewhere safe, perhaps near your altar or where you keep your crystals. Alternately, you can carry it with you to ward off liars and lying throughout your day.

## CHAPTER 11
# BLESSINGS

## SPELL JAR RECIPE #45: A GENERAL BLESSING SPELL JAR

*A recipe for general blessings on a special intention*

After cleansing your space, casting a spell circle if desired, and calling on any guides or intentions you feel drawn to, light a silver, gold, pink, or green spell candle with a match or lighter.

Then put the following ingredients in your jar:

- Sea salt, pink Himalayan salt, OR Epsom salts
- Amber, tiger's eye, OR citrine
- Selenite, clear quartz, OR moonstone
- Rose quartz, pearl, OR amethyst
- Basil, bay, OR rosemary
- Lemon, lavender, OR geranium oil
- Rose, geranium, OR ylang-ylang oil
- Special intention written on a slip of paper
- Silver, gold, pink, or green ribbon and a silver, gold, pink, or green candle for sealing

Seal the bottle with a stopper if desired, then cover the seal with green wax and a green ribbon. Hold the bottle in your hands for a few moments, feeling the energy and intuitively knowing that your special intention is blessed.

## SPELL JAR RECIPE #46: A SPELL FOR A BLESSING ON A HOME

*A recipe for blessing yours or someone else's home, perhaps when first moving in*

After cleansing your space, casting a spell circle if desired, and calling on any guides or intentions you feel drawn to, light a white, gold, or silver spell candle with a match or lighter.

Then put the following ingredients in your jar:

- Sea salt, pink Himalayan salt, OR Epsom salts
- Onyx, obsidian, OR hematite
- Black tourmaline, lavastone, OR shungite
- Selenite, howlite, OR clear quartz
- Basil, bay, OR rosemary
- Sage, chamomile, OR dandelion root
- Frankincense, cedarwood, OR myrrh oil
- Rose, geranium, OR ylang-ylang oil
- White, gold, or silver ribbon and a white, gold, or silver candle for sealing

Seal the bottle with a stopper if desired, then cover the seal with white, gold, or silver wax and a white, gold, or silver ribbon. Hold the bottle in your hands for a few moments, feeling the energy and saying something like:

*I bless this home*
*May it be safe, happy, and at peace*

*May the inhabitants live in joy and love*
*As long as may be*
*And so it is*

You can either keep it someplace safe or give it away to the proud owners of a new home.

## SPELL JAR RECIPE #47: A SPELL FOR A BLESSING ON A NEW BABY

*A recipe for blessing yours or someone else's new baby*

After cleansing your space, casting a spell circle if desired, and calling on any guides or intentions you feel drawn to, light a white, gold, or silver spell candle with a match or lighter.

Then put the following ingredients in your jar:

- Sea salt, pink Himalayan salt, OR Epsom salts
- Selenite, howlite, OR clear quartz
- Dill, coriander, OR fennel
- Elder, ivy, OR lilac
- Violet, chrysanthemum, OR rose
- Rose, geranium, OR ylang-ylang oil
- White, gold, or silver ribbon and a white, gold, or silver candle for sealing

Seal the bottle with a stopper if desired, then cover the seal with white, gold, or silver wax and a white, gold, or silver ribbon. Hold the bottle in your hands for a few moments, feeling the energy and pronouncing a blessing on the child. Use your intuition to know what to say, doing your best to choose words and phrases unique to that child's unique needs and circumstances. You can then either keep it someplace safe in your baby's room or give it to the new parents.

## SPELL JAR RECIPE #48: A SPELL FOR A BLESSING ON A CHILD BECOMING AN ADULT

*A recipe for blessing yours or someone else's child as they transition into adulthood (perhaps as a graduation gift or on their eighteenth birthday)*

After cleansing your space, casting a spell circle if desired, and calling on any guides or intentions you feel drawn to, light a white, gold, or silver spell candle with a match or lighter.

Then put the following ingredients in your jar:

- Sea salt, pink Himalayan salt, OR Epsom salts
- Selenite, howlite, OR clear quartz
- Jade, carnelian, OR jasper
- Garnet, diamond, ruby, emerald, OR sapphire
- Tiger's eye, citrine, OR pyrite
- Apple, apricot, OR banana (dried)
- Cashew OR walnut
- Frankincense, myrrh, OR cedarwood oil
- Tea tree, eucalyptus, OR cypress oil
- White, gold, or silver ribbon and a white, gold, or silver candle for sealing

Seal the bottle with a stopper if desired, then cover the seal with white, gold, or silver wax and a white, gold, or silver ribbon. Hold the bottle in your hands for a few moments, feeling the energy and pronouncing a blessing on the person. Use your intuition to know what to say, doing your best to choose words and phrases unique to that person's unique needs and circumstances. You can then give it to the person.

## SPELL JAR RECIPE #49: A SPELL FOR A BLESSING ON A PET

*A recipe for blessing and protecting your (or another's) pet*

After cleansing your space, casting a spell circle if desired, and calling on any guides or intentions you feel drawn to, light a black or white spell candle with a match or lighter.

Then put the following ingredients in your jar:

- Sea salt, pink Himalayan salt, OR Epsom salts
- Rice, amaranth, OR quinoa
- Black tourmaline, shungite, onyx, hematite, OR lavastone
- Rose quartz, amethyst, OR malachite
- Rosemary, parsley, OR sage
- Cedarwood, frankincense, OR myrrh oil
- Ylang-ylang, clary sage, OR orange oil
- A small piece of your pet's fur, feathers, or scales (alternately, you can use a small piece of their food, a piece of one of their old toys or collars, or a slip of paper with their name on it)
- Honey, sugar, OR maple syrup
- Black or white ribbon and a black or white candle for sealing

Seal the bottle with a stopper if desired, then cover the seal with black or white wax and a black or white ribbon. Hold the bottle in your hands for a few moments, feeling the energy and pronouncing a blessing on the pet. You can then keep the jar near your pet's food and water bowls or cage or pen (if the pet is yours) or give it to the owner of the pet.

## SPELL JAR RECIPE #50: A SPELL FOR A WISE AND PROSPEROUS NEW YEAR

*Did you know that the Wicca New Year is actually Samhain, which is on October 31$^{st}$? (Samhain is pronounced "sow-in"). Whether you celebrate New Year in October, January, or at the Chinese New Year...use this jar spell to set new intentions for the coming year, release the old, and re-center yourself in your witchcraft.*

After cleansing your space, casting a spell circle if desired, and calling on any guides or intentions you feel drawn to, light a gold or white spell candle with a match or lighter.

Then put the following ingredients in your jar:

- Sea salt, pink Himalayan salt, OR Epsom salts
- Rice, amaranth, OR quinoa
- Black tourmaline, shungite, onyx, hematite, OR lavastone
- Amethyst OR lepidolite
- Malachite OR bloodstone
- Selenite OR clear quartz
- Pyrite OR citrine
- Sage, thyme, OR rosemary
- Myrrh, frankincense, OR cedarwood oil
- A coin (for prosperity)
- Gold or white ribbon and a gold or white candle for sealing

Seal the bottle with a stopper if desired, then cover the seal with gold or white wax and a gold or white ribbon. Hold the bottle in your hands for a few moments, feeling the energy and repeating something like the following:

*As the old year dies*
*The new year is born*
*So the old self dies*
*And I am re-born*

You might wish to keep the jar someplace you can look at it throughout the year to help you keep any new year intentions you may be setting. Alternately, you can put it somewhere secret to let it do its work behind the scenes.

## SPELL JAR RECIPE #51: A SPELL FOR A BLESSING ON A NEW CAR

*A recipe to bless your new car (or the car of someone you know). Trucks, vans, and other vehicles are good, too.*

After cleansing your space, casting a spell circle if desired, and calling on any guides or intentions you feel drawn to, light a black or green spell candle with a match or lighter.

Then put the following ingredients in your jar:

- Sea salt, pink Himalayan salt, OR Epsom salts
- Nails, pins, OR thorns
- Black tourmaline, shungite, onyx, hematite, OR lavastone
- Selenite OR clear quartz
- Rose quartz OR amethyst
- Anise, parsley, OR garlic
- Dried eggshells, tree bark, OR small bits of a pinecone

- Eucalyptus, tea tree, OR peppermint oil
- Lemon, orange, OR lime oil
- Black or green ribbon and a black or green candle for sealing

Seal the bottle with a stopper if desired, then cover the seal with black or green wax and a black or green ribbon. Hold the bottle in your hands for a few moments, feeling the energy and repeating something like the following:

*I bless this vehicle*
*I bless the wheels and engine*
*I bless the seats and passengers... (etc.)*

Continue through each part of the vehicle, sending it love and light with your mind. Then you can keep the jar in the new car's glove box, underneath the seat, in the trunk, or anywhere out of the way (for safe driving!). And of course, you can also give it to the person it's for if it's for someone else's new car.

## SPELL JAR RECIPE #52: A SPELL FOR A BLESSING ON A WEDDING OR NEW MARRIAGE

*A recipe to bless yours or another's marriage, possibly as a wedding gift or for a couple's first house. As a side note, the Wiccan wedding ceremony is called "handfasting" and involves literally tying the couple's hands together. I think this is just so nice! I wish I'd known about it when my husband and I got married.*

After cleansing your space, casting a spell circle if desired, and calling on any guides or intentions you feel drawn to, light a red or white spell candle with a match or lighter.

Then put the following ingredients in your jar:

- Rice, amaranth, OR quinoa
- Sesame seeds OR sunflower seeds
- Selenite, howlite, OR clear quartz
- Diamond, garnet, OR opal
- Rose quartz OR amethyst
- Jade, lapis lazuli, OR malachite
- Calendula, chickweed, OR clover
- Cardamom, cumin, OR chili powder
- Licorice, nutmeg, OR red pepper
- Rose, jasmine, ylang-ylang, OR geranium oil
- Red or white ribbon and a red or white candle for sealing

Seal the bottle with a stopper if desired, then cover the seal with red or white wax and a red or white ribbon. Hold the bottle in your hands for a few moments, feeling the energy and repeating something like the following:

*To the happy couple,*
*May you be blessed*
*May you be prosperous and at peace*

You can then either keep the jar in a central place in your home (if it's for you and your partner) or give it to the happy couple!

## SPELL JAR RECIPE #53: A SPELL FOR A BLESSING ON A BIRTHDAY

*A recipe to bless your friend or loved one's coming year on their birthday*

After cleansing your space, casting a spell circle if desired, and calling on any guides or intentions you feel drawn to, light a silver, gold, or white spell candle with a match or lighter.

Then put the following ingredients in your jar:

- Rice, amaranth, OR quinoa
- Jade, jasper, OR aventurine
- Garnet, peridot, OR rhodochrosite
- Acorn, buckeye, OR chestnut
- Catnip, chicory, OR lemon balm
- Hibiscus, passionflower, OR honeysuckle
- Apple OR apricot (dried)
- Cardamom, cumin, OR chili powder
- Grapefruit, orange, OR tangerine oil
- Silver, gold, or white ribbon and a silver, gold, or white candle for sealing

Seal the bottle with a stopper if desired, then cover the seal with silver, gold, or white wax and a silver, gold, or white ribbon. Hold the bottle in your hands for a few moments, feeling the energy and repeating something like the following:

*To the dear one born on this day:*
*May you be blessed*
*May you be prosperous and at peace*

The jar is then ready to give to your friend or loved one on their birthday!

## CHAPTER 12
# CHAKRA HEALING SPELLS

**SPELL JAR RECIPE #54: ROOT CHAKRA HEALING SPELL**

*A recipe for healing the root chakra, which can improve health, abundance, balance, mental and emotional stability, connection to others, and goal setting*

After cleansing your space, casting a spell circle if desired, and calling on any guides or intentions you feel drawn to, light a red, brown, or black spell candle with a match or lighter.

Then put the following ingredients in your jar:

- Dirt, gravel, OR stones
- Black tourmaline, hematite, OR onyx
- Lavastone, shungite, OR obsidian
- Carnelian, ruby, OR bloodstone
- Potato, beet, OR carrot
- Dandelion root, ginger, OR coffee
- Bergamot, patchouli, OR petitgrain oil
- Cypress, spruce, OR cedarwood oil

- Root chakra affirmations written on a piece of paper
- Red, brown, or black ribbon and a red, brown, or black candle for sealing

Seal the bottle with a stopper if desired, then cover the seal with red, brown, or black wax and a red, brown, or black ribbon. Hold the bottle in your hands for a few moments, feeling the energy. If you choose, recite (out loud or in your mind) something like this:

*By sealing this jar I heal my root chakra*
*And so it is*

Keep the jar anywhere it can work its magic in the background, perhaps near your crystals or on your altar. You can also heal your root chakra by wearing red, brown, and black clothes, eating root vegetables and red or brown foods, working through ancestral and family trauma patterns, and grounding in nature.

## SPELL JAR RECIPE #55: SACRAL CHAKRA HEALING SPELL

*A recipe for healing the sacral chakra, which can improve creativity, relationships, romantic life, sexuality, fertility, the inner child, relationships with parents and parental figures, and healing from childhood trauma*

After cleansing your space, casting a spell circle if desired, and calling on any guides or intentions you feel drawn to, light an orange spell candle with a match or lighter.

Then put the following ingredients in your jar:

- Sea salt, pink Himalayan salt, OR Epsom salts

- Carnelian, jasper, OR citrine
- Cinnamon, cardamom, OR clove
- Ginger, turmeric, OR cumin
- Orange, lemon, OR lime oil
- Bergamot, patchouli, OR petitgrain oil
- Sandalwood, clary sage, OR lemongrass oil
- Ylang-ylang, geranium, OR jasmine oil
- Sacral chakra affirmations written on a piece of paper
- Orange ribbon and an orange candle for sealing

Seal the bottle with a stopper if desired, then cover the seal with orange wax and orange ribbon. Hold the bottle in your hands for a few moments, feeling the energy. If you choose, recite (out loud or in your mind) something like this:

*By sealing this jar I heal my sacral chakra*
*And so it is*

Keep the jar anywhere it can work its magic in the background, perhaps near your crystals or on your altar. You can also heal your sacral chakra by wearing orange clothes, eating orange foods and healthy fats, doing art, listening to music, journaling your feelings, taking a healing salt bath, getting a massage or Reiki session, writing a letter to your inner child, or talking to someone about your emotions.

## SPELL JAR RECIPE #56: SOLAR PLEXUS CHAKRA HEALING SPELL

*A recipe for healing the solar plexus chakra, which can improve confidence, decision making, boundary setting, digestion, balance, achievement, and inner strength*

After cleansing your space, casting a spell circle if desired, and calling on any guides or intentions you feel drawn to, light a yellow spell candle with a match or lighter.

Then put the following ingredients in your jar:

- Dirt, sand, OR salt
- Tiger's eye, pyrite, OR citrine
- Ginger, turmeric, OR cumin
- Chamomile, calendula, OR thistle
- Bergamot, patchouli, OR petitgrain oil
- Lemon, lime, OR lemongrass oil
- Solar plexus chakra affirmations written on a piece of paper
- Yellow ribbon and a yellow candle for sealing

Seal the bottle with a stopper if desired, then cover the seal with yellow wax and a yellow ribbon. Hold the bottle in your hands for a few moments, feeling the energy. If you choose, recite (out loud or in your mind) something like this:

*By sealing this jar, I heal my solar plexus chakra*
*And so it is*

Keep the jar anywhere it can work its magic in the background, perhaps near your crystals or on your altar. You can also heal your solar plexus chakra by wearing yellow clothes, eating yellow foods or carbohydrates, setting healthy boundaries, cutting out negativity from your life, making decisions and sticking to them, setting goals and making a plan to reach them, saying "no" to that which no longer serves you, exercising, and sunbathing.

## SPELL JAR RECIPE #57: HEART CHAKRA HEALING SPELL

*A recipe for healing the heart chakra, which can improve self-love, empathy, compassion, growth, support networks and communities, and heart and circulation issues*

After cleansing your space, casting a spell circle if desired, and calling on any guides or intentions you feel drawn to, light a green spell candle with a match or lighter.

Then put the following ingredients in your jar:

- Sea salt, pink Himalayan salt, OR Epsom salts
- Malachite, emerald, OR bloodstone
- Rose quartz, pearl, OR amethyst
- Fennel, rosemary, OR alfalfa
- Cypress, spruce, OR fennel oil
- Lime, lemongrass, OR eucalyptus oil
- Rose, geranium, OR ylang-ylang oil
- Heart chakra affirmations written on a piece of paper
- Green ribbon and a green candle for sealing

Seal the bottle with a stopper if desired, then cover the seal with green wax and a green ribbon. Hold the bottle in your hands for a few moments, feeling the energy. If you choose, recite (out loud or in your mind) something like this:

*By sealing this jar, I heal my heart chakra*
*And so it is*

Keep the jar anywhere it can work its magic in the background, perhaps near your crystals or on your altar. You can also heal your heart chakra by wearing green clothes, eating green leafy vegetables and other green foods, connecting with loved ones and communities, forgiving others, forest bathing, donating time or money or goods, practicing gratitude, and offering compassion and gentleness to yourself and others.

## SPELL JAR RECIPE #58: THROAT CHAKRA HEALING SPELL

*A recipe for healing the throat chakra, which can support healthy boundaries, truth telling, creativity and expression, public speaking, writing, clarity, and throat healing (such as thyroid and vocal cord issues)*

After cleansing your space, casting a spell circle if desired, and calling on any guides or intentions you feel drawn to, light a blue spell candle with a match or lighter.

Then put the following ingredients in your jar:

- Sea salt, pink Himalayan salt, OR Epsom salts
- Sodalite, aquamarine, OR lapis lazuli
- Blue lace agate, azurite, OR fluorite
- Peppermint, clary sage, OR eucalyptus oil
- Throat chakra affirmations written on a piece of paper
- Blue ribbon and a blue candle for sealing

Seal the bottle with a stopper if desired, then cover the seal with blue wax and a blue ribbon. Hold the bottle in your hands for a few moments, feeling the energy. If you choose, recite (out loud or in your mind) something like this:

*By sealing this jar, I heal my throat chakra*
*And so it is*

Keep the jar anywhere it can work its magic in the

background, perhaps near your crystals or on your altar. You can also heal your throat chakra by wearing blue clothes, eating blue foods and lots of liquids along with foods from the sea (including fish and seaweed), journaling about your thoughts and feelings, creating art or music or literature or other creative endeavors, updating your wardrobe or hairstyle, trying new things, speaking your truth, and exploring what it means to be your true self.

## SPELL JAR RECIPE #59: THIRD EYE CHAKRA HEALING SPELL

*A recipe for healing the third eye chakra, which can improve intuition, wisdom, knowledge and learning, mental health, focus, clarity, sleep, and dreams*

After cleansing your space, casting a spell circle if desired, and calling on any guides or intentions you feel drawn to, light a purple spell candle with a match or lighter.

Then put the following ingredients in your jar:

- Sea salt, pink Himalayan salt, OR Epsom salts
- Amethyst, sapphire, topaz, OR lepidolite
- Basil, rosemary, OR bay
- Lavender, clary sage, OR frankincense oil
- Third eye chakra affirmations written on a piece of paper
- Purple ribbon and a purple candle for sealing

Seal the bottle with a stopper if desired, then cover the seal with purple wax and a purple ribbon. Hold the bottle in your hands for a few moments, feeling the energy. If you choose, recite (out loud or in your mind) something like this:

*By sealing this jar, I heal my third eye chakra*
*And so it is*

Keep the jar anywhere it can work its magic in the background, perhaps near your crystals or on your altar. You can also heal your third eye chakra by wearing purple or indigo blue clothes, eating purple and dark blue foods (such as blueberries, acai, goji berries, purple carrots, eggplant, purple cabbage, etc.), meditating, doing yoga, practicing intuition, detoxing, chanting, and breathwork.

## SPELL JAR RECIPE #60: CROWN CHAKRA HEALING SPELL

*A recipe for healing the crown chakra, which can improve spiritual connection and insights, mental health, peace, serenity, calm, sleep, dreams, and knowing your soul's purpose*

After cleansing your space, casting a spell circle if desired, and calling on any guides or intentions you feel drawn to, light a white or purple spell candle with a match or lighter.

Then put the following ingredients in your jar:

- Sea salt, pink Himalayan salt, OR Epsom salts
- Amethyst, fluorite, OR lepidolite
- Selenite, clear quartz, OR howlite
- Cedarwood, myrrh, OR frankincense oil
- Crown chakra affirmations written on a piece of paper
- White or purple ribbon and a white or purple candle for sealing

Seal the bottle with a stopper if desired, then cover the seal with purple wax and a purple ribbon. Hold the bottle in your hands for a few moments, feeling the energy. If you choose, recite (out loud or in your mind) something like this:

*By sealing this jar, I heal my crown chakra*
*And so it is*

Keep the jar anywhere it can work its magic in the background, perhaps near your crystals or on your altar. You can also heal your third eye chakra by wearing purple clothes, eating purple and white foods, fasting and detoxing, meditating (or praying if you're into it), joining a spiritual practice or group, getting clear on your soul's purpose, learning about philosophy or culture, giving to or serving others, taking a salt bath, spending time in the fresh air, and reading.

# About the Author

Allegra Grant is a writer, lecturer, teacher, and coach living in New York City with her husband and their rescue dog, Cliff.

Allegra's interest in the metaphysical and "new age" arts goes back years and was born out of her attraction to one crystal, a Blue Lace Agate. When she allowed the crystal to affect her life, a whole world of possibilities opened up. And with years of research, interviewing experts, and personal trial-and-error under her belt, Allegra began to share what she had learned.

You can visit Allegra Grant's author page on Amazon to see her other books. Or scan this QR code:

https://www.amazon.com/Allegra-Grant/e/B09D1WP3MK

Allegra believes that when you allow yourself to experience the wonders of the universe... literally, nothing is impossible.

# INGREDIENTS GLOSSARY

HERBS & PLANTS

**Acorn:** Luck, abundance, wisdom, protection, grounding
**African violet:** Protection, spiritual strength, harmony, love, happiness, gentleness
**Alfalfa:** Luck, prosperity, money, healing, cleansing
**Allspice:** Money, success, courage, good fortune, winning, happiness
**Almond:** Wisdom, prosperity, money, healing
**Aloe:** Healing, protection, affection, luck, support
**Amaranth:** Healing, abundance
**Angelica:** Protection, harmony, spiritual connection
**Anise:** Cleansing, purifying, youth, wealth, good fortune, protection, safety
**Apple:** Wisdom, knowledge, love, friendship, growth, longevity, youth, beauty
**Apricot:** Love, friendship, healing, happiness
**Arrowroot:** Purification, healing

# INGREDIENTS GLOSSARY

**Astragalus:** Energy, protection, shielding, clarity, concentration
**Avocado:** Beauty, love, passion, glamor
**Bamboo:** Protection, clarity, luck, safety
**Banana:** Fertility, potency, prosperity
**Barley:** Protection, love, healing, abundance
**Basil:** Concentration, mental acuity, trust, confidence, love, communication, honesty
**Bay:** Protection, clarity, positivity, abundance, clairvoyance
Beans (various): Protection, abundance, love
**Beet:** Grounding, abundance, love
**Birch:** Protection, purification, cleansing
**Black pepper:** Banishment, protection, security, safety, cleansing, strength
**Blackberry:** Protection, healing, money, happiness
**Bladderwrack:** Cleansing, protection, healing, money, psychic abilities
**Blueberry:** Protection, healing, abundance, truth telling
**Buckeye:** Luck, money, wealth, abundance
**Burdock:** Cleansing, protection, purification, positivity
**Cabbage:** Fertility, good luck, money, success
**Cactus:** Protection, safety, chastity
**Calendula:** Protection, dreams, psychic abilities, fidelity, positivity, justice
**Camellia:** Riches
**Camphor:** Dreams, psychic abilities, love
**Caraway:** Protection, mental powers, cleansing, health, healing
**Cardamom:** Love, fidelity, cleansing, persuasion, abundance, attraction
**Carnation:** Healing, protection, strength, love
**Carrot:** Grounding, abundance, fertility
**Cashew:** Money, success

# INGREDIENTS GLOSSARY

**Catnip:** Protection, attraction, beauty, happiness, joy, love
**Cayenne:** Protection, healing, cleansing, positivity, courage
**Cedar:** Protection, cleansing, abundance, mental clarity, purity, safety, strength, power
**Celery:** Cleansing, psychic powers, fertility, virility
**Chamomile:** Sleep, love, meditation, protection, tranquility, peace
**Cherry:** Money, positivity, growth, happiness, love
**Chestnut:** Abundance, money, wealth
**Chia:** Protection, health
**Chickweed:** Abundance, protection, fidelity, healing, fertility
**Chicory:** Joy, love, happiness, digestion, healing
**Chili pepper:** Sensuality, romance, passion, drive, stamina, fidelity
**Chives:** Protection, cleansing, weight loss
**Chrysanthemum:** Protection
**Cilantro:** Mental acuity, attraction, communication, creativity
**Cinnamon:** Love, passion, psychic powers, money, wealth, success, creativity, attraction
**Clove:** Positivity, protection, money, psychic powers, healing, clarity, success
**Clover:** Money, love, success, abundance, protection, fidelity
**Coffee:** Grounding, friendship, strength
**Coriander:** Healing, cleansing, purifying, love, health, peace
**Cumin:** Protection, safety, love, fidelity, peace, clarity
**Dandelion:** Healing, wishes, purification, positivity
**Dandelion root:** Grounding, protection, dreams, healing
**Dill:** Protection, purity, abundance, health, weight loss, digestion

## INGREDIENTS GLOSSARY

**Echinacea:** Healing, psychic abilities, money, fertility, protection
**Elder:** Protection, beauty, healing, prosperity, safety, sleep
**Fennel:** Communication, confidence, courage, strength, creativity, purification
**Flax:** Money, protection, abundance, healing, beauty
**Garlic:** Healing, protection, safety, security, cleansing, digestion, luck
**Ginger:** Healing, money, cleansing, digestion, success, purification, balance, grounding
**Gum Arabic:** Spirituality, purity, healing, positivity
**Hazel:** Mental abilities, protection, wisdom, luck
**Heather:** Protection, weather
**Hibiscus:** Love, passion, friendship, romance
**Honeysuckle:** Love, friendship, healing, relationships
**Horehound:** Protection, mental clarity, focus, creativity, balance
**Horseradish:** Protection, virility, passion
**Ivy:** Protection, fertility, healing
**Lavender:** Calm, wisdom, compassion, healing, dreams, cleansing
**Lemon:** Purification, happiness, friendship, love, joy
**Lemon balm:** Love, success, healing, calm
**Lemongrass:** Positivity, clarity, healing, protection, love, passion, friendship
**Licorice:** Love, protection, attraction, passion, fidelity
**Lilac:** Peace, harmony, protection, wisdom, memory, luck
**Lime:** Protection, purification, healing, luck
**Mint:** Communication, healing, protection, abundance, happiness, calm
**Mistletoe:** Love, passion, abundance, reconciliation, protection, creativity, attraction

**Mustard:** Acceptance, courage, happiness, strength, awareness, faith, endurance
**Nettle:** Protection, positivity
**Nutmeg:** Luck, prosperity, abundance, clairvoyance, fidelity
**Oak:** Purification, protection, strength, prosperity
**Onion:** Protection, purification, healing, cleansing
**Orange:** Love, joy, purification, wealth, abundance, luck, happiness, positivity
**Oregano:** Peace, healing, cleansing, happiness, health
**Palo santo:** Cleansing, healing, protection, open mind, positivity, strength
**Parsley:** Healing, protection, safety, prosperity, communication, truth
**Passionflower:** Friendship, passion, attraction, positivity, peace, calm, sleep
**Plantain:** Fertility, abundance, healing, protection, strength
**Red pepper:** Emotional support, fidelity, friendship, self-esteem, longevity
**Rose:** Love, calm, passion, romance, healing
**Rosemary:** Protection, healing, clarity, purity, love, concentration, intellect, cleansing
**Sage:** Clarity, sanctity, wisdom, protection, purity, balance, grounding, luck
**Sandalwood:** Protection, peace, awareness, meditation
**Sesame:** Healing, fertility, creativity, money, abundance, luck, success
**St. John's wort:** Calm, sleep, health, protection, strength, happiness
**Strawberry:** Love, beauty, luck, happiness
**Sunflower:** Positivity, grounding, happiness, protection, stamina, power

# INGREDIENTS GLOSSARY

**Tarragon:** Confidence, self-esteem, happiness
**Thistle:** Protection, purification
**Thyme:** Purification, courage, healing, love, psychic abilities, cleansing, focus, memory
**Valerian:** Purification, protection, sleep, love, calm
**Vanilla:** Love, passion, romance, creativity
**Vetiver:** Money, love, protection, grounding
**Walnut:** Healing, grounding, purification
**Willow:** Communication, eloquence, healing, love
**Yarrow:** Healing, protection, courage, marriage, strength, confidence
**Yellow dock:** Releasing, fertility, grounding

## CRYSTALS

**Agate:** Strength, courage, protection, healing, balance, grounding, optimism
**Amazonite:** Emotions, healing, communication, truth, creativity, psychic abilities
**Amber:** Healing, protection, peace, abundance, focus, money, clarity, confidence
**Amethyst:** Intuition, healing, protection, peace, psychic abilities, beauty
**Aquamarine:** Communication, creativity, clarity, peace, tolerance, cleansing, compassion
**Aventurine:** Luck, money, healing, prosperity, balance, harmony, success
**Azurite:** Truth, intuition, kindness, mental abilities, strength, courage, patience, peace
**Beryl:** Guidance, acceptance, balance, confidence, courage
Black tourmaline: Grounding, strength, stability, sleep

**Bloodstone:** Healing, money, courage, fertility, balance, concentration, trust
**Blue lace agate:** Communication, intuition, creativity
**Carnelian:** Success, joy, balance, creativity, power, abundance, money, passion
**Citrine:** Abundance, willpower, money, positivity, success, happiness, growth
**Clear quartz:** Clarity, purity, cleansing
**Diamond:** Clarity, honesty, protection, cleansing, focus, fidelity
**Emerald:** Healing, cleansing, friendship, happiness, fidelity
**Fluorite:** Mental clarity, focus, concentration, intuition, balance, grounding
**Garnet:** Happiness, fidelity, friendship, healing, balance, calm, love, relationships
**Hematite:** Grounding, balancing, support, stability, strength, protection, boundaries
**Howlite:** Sleep, peace, calm, communication
**Jade:** Wealth, prosperity, success, luck, friendship, harmony
**Jasper:** Success, abundance, luck, strength, comfort, protection, safety, healing, peace
**Lapis lazuli:** Intuition, communication, healing, wisdom, joy, peace, fidelity, protection
**Lavastone:** Strength, grounding, sleep, balance
**Lepidolite:** Sleep, calm, peace, spiritual connection, psychic abilities
**Malachite:** Healing, love, connection, trauma release, opening, fidelity, peace
**Moonstone:** Peace, spiritual growth, connection, harmony, joy, calm, balance
**Obsidian:** Protection, grounding, healing, safety, balance, overcoming, strength

## INGREDIENTS GLOSSARY

**Onyx:** Protection, strength, endurance, courage, power, grounding

**Opal:** Peace, love, hope, fidelity, communication, power

**Pearl:** Peace, calm, rejuvenation, cleansing, purity, love, healing

**Peridot:** Calm, peace, relaxation, friendship, healing, growth, balance

**Pyrite:** Abundance, wealth, money, willpower, strength, luck, confidence

**Rhodochrosite:** Harmony, friendship, compassion, kindness

**Rose Quartz:** Love, self-love, compassion, harmony, peace, balance

**Selenite:** Aura cleansing, protection, healing, clarity, purification, balance

**Shungite:** Grounding, sleep, purification, protection, clarity

**Sodalite:** Truth, communication, wisdom, healing, calm, self-esteem, intuition

**Tiger's eye:** Luck, power, strength, confidence, protection, courage, wealth

**Turquoise:** Communication, health, creativity, protection, peace

**Ruby:** Love, healing, passion, compassion, balance

**Topaz:** Intuition, knowledge, concentration, balance, healing

**Sapphire:** Wisdom, memory, mental clarity, balance, focus, concentration, positivity

## OILS

**Bergamot:** Positivity, calm, abundance balancing, healing, grounding, emotional release

# INGREDIENTS GLOSSARY

**Cedarwood:** Protection, grounding, purification, healing, balance

**Cinnamon:** Wealth, abundance, cleansing, psychic abilities, focus, healing, love

**Clary sage:** Cleansing, protection, grounding, wisdom, balancing, longevity

**Clove:** Positivity, courage, protection, productivity, wealth, luck

**Cypress:** Healing, emotional release, sleep, growth, balance, energy

**Eucalyptus:** Cleansing, healing, growth, clarity, emotional release, positivity, peace, focus

**Fennel:** Courage, healing, cleansing, purification, digestion

**Frankincense:** Cleansing, peace, protection, clarity, healing, sleep, intuition, wisdom

**Geranium:** Love, calm, passion, romance, creativity, balance, harmony

**Ginger:** Healing, positivity, abundance, digestion, clarity, gratitude, happiness, courage

**Grapefruit:** Harmony, friendship, positivity, cooperation, purification, healing

**Jasmine:** Passion, romance, peace, love, healing, serenity, creativity, grace

**Juniper berry:** Healing, sleep, grounding, balance, harmony, protection

**Lavender:** Calm, peace, meditation, sleep, healing

**Lemon:** Happiness, joy, peace, friendship, cleansing, healing, love, awareness

**Lemongrass:** Energy, positivity, cleansing, calm, happiness

**Lime:** Cheerfulness, positivity, cleansing, purification, protection, healing

**Mandarin:** Happiness, friendship, positivity, cleansing, purification, clarity

## INGREDIENTS GLOSSARY

**Melissa:** Calm, happiness, peace, positivity, sleep
**Myrrh:** Healing, cleansing, protection, spirituality, psychic abilities
**Neroli:** Love, positivity, calm, passion, romance, happiness, purification
**Niaouli:** Protection, cleansing, healing
**Palmarosa:** Healing, peace, serenity, positivity, love
**Patchouli:** Grounding, attraction, money, passion, positivity, healing, focus, success
**Peppermint:** Excitement, motivation, digestion, peace, tranquility, focus, clarity, protection
**Petitgrain:** Calm, healing, balance, grounding
**Rose:** Love, passion, calm, romance, healing, positivity, happiness
**Rosemary:** Healing, cleansing, psychic abilities, knowing, insight, focus
**Sandalwood:** Purification, comfort, healing, protection, positivity, release, awareness
**Spruce:** Grounding, balancing, healing
**Sweet Orange:** Joy, peace, friendship, happiness, positivity, comfort, warmth, luck, success
**Tangerine:** Positivity, friendship, happiness, calm, energy
**Tea Tree:** Cleansing, protection, purifying, healing, clarity, calm
**Thyme:** Cleansing, courage, achievement, healing, positivity, concentration, clarity
**Vanilla:** Happiness, passion, creativity, love, positivity, calm
**Vetiver:** Balance, grounding, harmony, sleep, mental clarity, focus
**Ylang-ylang:** Peace, love, passion, excitement, harmony, calm, romance, spirituality, gratitude

# RESOURCES

https://www.youtube.com/watch?v=zDW5bxsrsqw
https://www.youtube.com/watch?v=ybsS0nu8kFE
https://spells8.com/printable-pages-book-shadows/?gclid=CjwKCAjww8mWBhABEiwAl6-2RcswlQ7qUTMWZdhb7lupKksg9AFuMWaNNpHHUD_tpT1hdwWe6Z_ItRoCKwEQAvD_BwE
https://exemplore.com/wicca-witchcraft/Witchcraft-for-Beginners-How-to-Cast-a-Jar-Spell
https://www.google.com/url?sa=t&rct=j&q=&esrc=s&source=web&cd=&ved=2ahUKEwjr9I-H517j6AhWBj4kEHaueATc4FBAWegQI-BRAB&url=https%3A%2F%2Fwww.bop.gov%2Ffoia%2Fdocs%2Fwiccamanual.pdf&usg=AOvVaw2ADSo81uwazgzkpShNGX6h
https://sheroserevolution.com/shanijay/spell-jars-self-love-protection-abundance/
https://www.learnreligions.com/basic-principles-of-wicca-2562829
https://www.refinery29.com/en-us/real-witches-wiccan-religion-beliefs
https://www.brandeis.edu/now/2021/september/wicca-berger-conversation.html
https://web.mit.edu/pipa/www/rede.html
https://www.learnreligions.com/the-wiccan-rede-2562601
https://wiccanow.com/protection-jar-spell/
https://wiccanow.com/how-to-cast-a-spell-a-foolproof-guide/
https://magickalspot.com/making-a-protection-spell-jar/
https://witchjournal.com/protection-spell-jar/
https://witchyspiritualstuff.com/witchcraft-spells-getting-rid-of-someone/
https://www.learnreligions.com/jar-spells-in-folk-magic-2562516
https://eclecticwitchcraft.com/how-to-make-a-protection-jar-ingredients-spell/
https://tarotpugs.com/2019/06/07/banishing-negativity-jar-spell/
https://averyhart.co/blog/2016/12/21/banishing
https://tipofthemoon.store/spells/spell-jars

## RESOURCES

https://witchjournal.com/protection-spell-jar/
https://spells8.com/banishing-spells/
https://www.spellsofmagic.com/spells/spiritual_spells/banishing_spells/page.html
https://magickalspot.com/banishing-spells/
https://www.tumblr.com/becomingwitchy/169705228397/spells-and-sigils-for-animals-pets-and-familiars
https://www.holidayinsights.com/halloween/witchcal.htm
https://lancasteronline.com/features/faith_values/wiccans-celebrate-pagan-new-year/article_0c279b38-37bc-500e-acb0-ddf83e05f551.html

**Essential Oil Resources:**
https://agirlworthsaving.net/an-introduction-to-magical-essential-oils/
https://otherworldlyoracle.com/essential-oil-magical-properties-chart/
https://pranachic.com/blogs/blog/essential-oils-and-their-properties
https://www.enchantedaromatics.com/15-magical-properties-of-essential-oils/
https://www.thewholesomewitch.com/essential-oils-magical-uses/
https://medium.com/witchology-magazine/magickal-oils-101-1caaf88bb61d

**Herbs:**
https://www.thewiccanlady.co.uk/herbal-grimoire
A Writer's Guide to Potion and Spell Ingredients Used in Magic - HobbyLark
A Complete List of Herbs and Their Magickal Uses – The Thrifty Witch School
Herbal Lore Archives - darkoct02
https://attichaos.tumblr.com/post/686679517878747136/p2-common-herbs-a-z
Green witch herb guide! These are the plants I use and have written in my grimoire : r/witchcraft
~Small Herbal Grimoire~
Herbal Grimoire A-Z - askanthony

# RESOURCES

https://dzenwitch.tumblr.com/post/181616631663/gemstones-their-meanings-40-stones-for-magick

https://thequeensgrimoire.tumblr.com/post/164025916369/stir-by-still-crystals-their-correspondences

Magical Herbal Correspondences

Common Herbs and their Uses — Bodhi Basics

Tables of Magickal Correspondences | Light Warriors Legion

A Witch's glossary of herbs – Grove and Grotto

**Crystals:**

Using Crystals and Gemstones in Magic

Crystal Correspondences – The Most Comprehensive Guide Ever – Wicca Now – Everything You Need To Know About Wicca

Crystal Correspondence A to Z / Alles over Edelstenen / Blog | Heketa

**Candles:**

https://www.learnreligions.com/introduction-to-candle-magic-2561684

**Moon Phases:**

https://www.allure.com/story/moon-phases-magic-spells

https://www.thehoodwitch.com/timing-spells-by-the-moon

http://witchipedia.wikidot.com/main:spell-timing

**Magic Circles:**

https://www.thenotsoinnocentsabroad.com/blog/how-to-cast-a-wicca-ritual-magic-circle

https://www.thefrenchwitch.shop/blogs/infos/how-to-cast-a-magical-circle

https://thesirenlppacs.com/1123/witchy-wednesdays/how-to-cast-a-circle/

For spells, do I have to cast a circle? - Quora

Should you always cast a circle when preparing for a spell? - Quora

**Brooms and Cleansing:**

https://whimsysoul.com/how-to-cleanse-a-space-energetically-and-spiritually/

Printed in Great Britain
by Amazon